White Trash
&
Southern

~~~~~

Collected Poems, Volume 1

~~~~~

C.S. Fuqua

For Bonnie and Tegan
and those who inspired these poems.

We'll walk into this one again and again....

Contents

Becoming

Carnalities

Coupled

Relativity

Acquainted

Rosé Tinted Glasses

Dementia

Amen

Coda

Acknowledgements

Grateful acknowledgement to the following publications where the majority of these poems first appeared: *Abbey, Amelia, The Archer, The Armchair Aesthete, The Autumn Sound, Blank Gun Silencer, Backspace, The Blind Man'S Rainbow, The Blotter, Blue Light Review, Bogg, Bottomfish, CaKe, A Journal OF Poetry & Art, Cellar Roots, Chili Verde Review, Chiron Review, Chopper Journal, Chrysalis, Coal City Review, Cokefish, Conceit Magazine, Confetti, A Contemporary American Survey*: *The Unitarian-Universalist Poets, The Contemporary Review, Cube Literary Magazine, Curbside Review, Daring Poetry Quarterly, Devil Blossoms, Doggerel, Draconian Measures, Edgz, Elk River Review, Empirical Magazine, Erete's Bloom, Fauquier Poetry Journal, Fennel Stalk, Gertrude, The Green Muse, Haight Ashbury Literary Journal, The Higginsville Reader, Hunger Magazine, Illuminations, Impetus, In Concert, Inky Blue, Iodine, James River Review, Just West of Athens, Lactuca, Late Knocking, Leapings, Lime Green Bulldozers, Main Channel Voices, Main Street Rag, Metropolis, Miller's Pond, Mind in Motion, Minnesota Ink, Mobius, The Muse, Oak Square, Oasis, Odin's Eye, Omnific, Onionhead Literary Quarterly, Oxygen, Paisley Moon, The Paper Salad Poetry Journal, Pearl, Piedmont Literary Review, Pinehurst Journal, Poet Magazine, Poetic Voices, Poetry Forum, The Poetry Peddler, The Pointed Circle, Powhatan Review, Protea Poetry Journal, Proof Rock, Raw Bone, RE:AL, The Journal of Liberal Arts, Red Dancefloor, River King, River Poets Journal, samizdada, The Screech Owl, Seedhouse, Sierra Nevada College Review, Sisyphus, Slipstream, Snow Monkey, Spirits, Stuff, SubtleTea, Sulphur River Literary Review, Thirteen Poetry Magazine, Thorny Locust, Tipton Poetry Journal, Tight, Tripwire, The Triskelion, Twisted, U.S. 1 Worksheets, Up Against The Wall Mother, The Vein Literary Magazine, Veil, Vice Versa, The Village Idiot, Wilderness House Review, Williwaw,* and *Zuzu's Petals Quarterly*.

Many thanks to Rick Kennett of Cooperative Ink for his editorial assistance.

I am indebted to all who contributed through experience or assistance, by design or accident. Rick asked if the poems within are autobiographical. Yes. No. All of the poems evolved out of experience, but that doesn't mean the events in the poems transpired as detailed. Some did. Some didn't. Some sort of. Many of the ideas came from other people. Some poems are simple exercises of placing myself in other people's situations. An idea has a way of becoming more on the page, transforming into something completely different from the original inspiration and intent. Don't believe anything you read. Believe everything.

Thank you, Bonnie and Tegan. Who could ask for more...?

Finally, I am deeply grateful to you, the reader, for buying this book. I hope you find some part of it worthwhile and entertaining.

Those days are gone forever

Studebaker

There, next to the polished Mercedes,
the yellow Studebaker,
rust holes in the fender walls,
paint-chipped hood,
worn seats—nothing like
the old man's.
He kept his sparkling, let me tell you,
just like the Model T before,
and the Thunderbird, the '56 Chevy,
and the entire freeway of cars
that sped through my youth,
but none was so striking
as that hand-buffed Studebaker
with its white walls,
its custom steering wheel,
its immaculate seats,

and that night,
coming back from Andalusia
when they thought I was asleep
in the back,
and he reached over,
grabbed her hair,
jerked her hard enough
to spin her head to the side.
I found two spots of dried blood
the following day,
and I remembered how the moon
had hung in the rear window
just below a cluster of stars
as he muttered, Christ,
why'd you make me do that?
And she had rested her head
back against that perfect seat
as the hum of new tires on asphalt
rose through the floorboard.

Holes

It remains a hole, nothing
more than a description
of a few moments,
thirty years after the fact.
The music's twang led him
into the doorway. His father
changed shirts, shaved,
slapped on cologne.
His mother demanded answers.
The record skipped as the boy flattened,
his mother and father passing him as though he was
part of the wall. An ashtray shattered through
the front window, and the boy cupped his hands
over his ears, forcing screams into hollow echoes.

He is no fool, this boy, this man. He needs
no memory to know what came next.
But that hole, that darkness—
that's where reasons lie, he's certain,
and yet his suit is dirty,
his stomach rumbles,
and tomorrow he must look for work.

~~~~~

1963

The limb shudders:
he points his toes
and dreams of soaring.

Foul wind sears leaves
off quivering branches.
His daddy's laugh rings from inside:
Blew that nigger-lover's brains out.

Television faces,
passing short glimpses:
camera tracks.

3

Cool wind dusts
play period.
Chains grind against
bare steel bars.

The black boy says
his mama cried.
The white boy's face burns.

They point their toes,
wishing to touch the sky,
to soar free of the force that
snares, pulls them back.

~~~~~

Trusting B.J.

Only a lawn mower,
its blade removed
for safe repair.
And he's there, uncle B.J.,
the chips man,
the extra quarter man,
the *gooser* when you're not
expecting to laugh.
He sets the choke,
says, Okay now, grab it.
And the boy takes the nipple
between forefinger and thumb
as B.J. pulls the crank cord,
smoke spewing gray and cloudy,
the plug seizing, jolting.
B.J.'s laughing as the boy
finally snaps free.
The boy settles on a Coke crate
and watches B.J.
adjust the points,
replace the plug,
resurrect the engine.
B.J. tosses the old plug
toward the boy,

and the boy flinches back.
B.J. laughs. It won't bite.
The boy reaches for the plug,
jumps as B.J. shouts, "Gotcha."
The boy rises from the crate,
backs away slowly
as B.J. bolts on the blade.

~~~~~

For Cathy, Growing

A century later,
she carries herself
with diverted eyes
and sagging shoulders,
as is customary in this town.

I see her in the mill
on the opposite side
of a corn-stuffed sack
twice our size,
grunting and giggling
as we drag it to Big Daddy
to feed the roaring machine.

Later, she's whispering
during afternoon naptime,
Big Mama's asleep.
We swing out of bed, into the shed,
and she squats in a corner
on the dirt floor
while I sneak peeks
as I watch for Big Mama
who could barrel out of the house
at any time with switch in hand.
Then we're bouncing
into the truck bed,
bumping open the tailgate,
my nose beating the bumper.
She holds my head back,
smiling, kissing my brow.

With pee streaking her pants,
blood speckling my shirt,
we creep back

a century ago
in silence,
as is customary in this town.

~~~~~

Churning

I can't picture anything between that old woman's legs
but the wooden churn, the handle working up and down,
up and down. She rose at dawn to fill the kitchen
with scents of bacon and biscuits, then she'd gather eggs
while the old man's hands trembled, the cup spilling
black coffee into a sipping saucer. She swept and dusted
and shelled peas and read the Bible as if God spoke
only to her through those dead men's words. She fished
afternoons while the old man napped. He never knew
she fed most of the catch to wild cats.

Saturdays she churned milk into butter and spread it
on Sunday biscuits that oozed melted cheese.
The woman died a quarter-century before the old man.
I can't say what he did with the churn,
but he sold the cows, killed the chickens,
let the weeds take the garden, ate packaged pork,
gave the Bible to his youngest son.
On summer afternoons, a grandkid fed bream
to cats hissing in the undergrowth.

~~~~~

The Following Days

In the days that followed the final night,
I don't remember much until
she placed the plants in the backseat,
clothes in the trunk,

6

and set the sewing machine in my lap,
cushioned by pants she'd sewn on that machine.
Pine sweetened the air
and though it was winter, I remember warmth.
No goodbyes to my father,
the time chosen specifically for that convenience.
The following days passed as days pass—
new kid in school, jokes,
fading, moving on beyond the life
that she chose to cling to.
She begged on his few visits
for another try, another go at what never was,
and I watched the bruises yellow and fade,
watered the plants, nurtured new shoots,
and bought factory-made jeans, blended.

~~~~~

Hidden Inside

So they've drawn the curtain,
tied their voices
and she's even left the house.

Where's the boy?
The girl?

(Two more years,
I hit the road.)

(An ashtray—
no,
no,
it was a rock,
when she was mowing...)

Good summer explanations cower
under beds of autumn frost
when idle mowers sling no stones.

I heard the glass shatter,
the voices scream.

And though the curtain's drawn,
the jagged shards glisten
here on the outside.

~~~~~

Home Movies

Frame by frame, she steps up behind him,
her hand going to the top of his head,
pressing playfully down;
then he's rising for battle,
but the camera cuts to another scene,
another year, and the sons are grouping
with their wives and children for still shots
as she bobs her hip into his, and he's spinning
to her, anger twisting his face,
his arms dropping the boy to the ground;
then the screen flashes white,
but the boy still feels the grass under his feet,
cool and damp in the August heat,
the clip of Daddy's knee against his head,
an accident, yet he curls, crying,
hears Mama's voice,
I was playing, honey, just playing.
Others are moving away,
stealing glimpses over their shoulders
as Daddy's oldest brother turns Daddy aside.
Mama lifts the boy into her arms,
shushing him: *Don't be a baby.*
Hushpuppies crackle in deep grease
as Mama presses into the group,
whispering to another in-law,
I just don't know what gets into him.

In the hiss of the tape rewinding,
the boy hears their voices echo,
their threats to leave, to kill.
He stretches out on the thick carpet,
pretending the plush pile
is summer's damp grass
as he gropes for the remote.

8

At 12

Peeking into the kitchen
when Mama was asleep,
when I should've been,
I watched Daddy in dim light
wash himself at the sink.

Thanksgiving: they put me on a bus
to Mama's sister's—
a treat, they said,
with indoor plumbing.
My bedroom there leaked
into an empty hallway.

At home: he'd enclosed
the back porch,
stuck pipes up
through the floor.
A hole had broken
through the kitchen wall
into the living room—
an accident, Mama told me,
and Daddy rose from the table, his meal
unfinished.

Daddy put a toilet in the porch room
and said he would install a tub.
It never came.
I peeked around my door till late winter
when Mama and I moved to her sister's.
Daddy washed himself every night
in thin light bleeding in from
the living room, coiling around
his manhood.

~~~~~

Hunchback

He recalls most pool at the river bar
where we played eight ball

9

while the hunchback served us
icy Cokes and cold Buds.
I don't know where my mother
was then, but I have ideas.
The boy gas-jockey and his old man:
We shot pool every night
those last two months,
after work, those ten-hour
days broken by Madeline's
synthetic grins directed at me
until she could slip away with him.

The hunchback never spoke
as far as I know, only grunted
when anyone addressed him.
Dad said he was crazy,
but not as crazy as marriage.
The week before my mother's
accusations sent Dad
into a rage of fists,
someone found the hunchback
in the bar's backroom bed,
five bullets in his chest.
Cops said he killed himself.
Dad says those days were
the best he ever spent with me.

~~~~~

Last Date

It's like a swing,
she tells her boy,
swaying back and forth
to the ring of
Floyd Cramer's magic.
She lolls her head,
eyes closed, croons,
I could've been a singer
if not for Mama and your daddy…
She bites her lip,
rocks like a baby

on the downside of daylight,
dreaming of applause
and romance, recalling *Mama*'s
callused hand holding hers,
the raspy whisper,
It'll be all right.

She drops to her knees,
resets the needle,
then glides around her son,
cooing, *I could have*
been a dancer. Stars
glitter beyond the pane,
and the boy wonders
if the woman
his father took
dances to the same
songs as his mother.

~~~~~

Lunch

Dad never denied
his unfaithfulness
except at lunch,
when, spitting chicken and peas,
he'd yell from the table,
"Your mama says
I'm a whore hopper."

"You'd better fall
on your knees,"
Mama would warn,
"and beg God to forgive you."

Dad now makes his bed with the one
I sometimes saw
in his office afternoons,
smoking,
pinching my cheeks,
asking how my "Good Mama's doin',

God bless her."

Dad tells me
God's been good to him.
Mom asks me
what she did wrong,
wonders why
God is deaf.

~~~~~

Waves

Waves wash onto sand,
finely white as processed sugar,
and the boy emerges,
twisting, clawing, screaming,
jelly stingers
sliding over his body,
mother grabbing him,
snatching him,
trying not to touch
those slimy tendrils.
Do something,
do something, she cries.
The father laughs,
breaks a cigarette in half,
smears tobacco over the welts,
tells the boy to grow up,
grow up, act like a man.

Mother, father walk away,
and the boy picks at
the cigarette butt,
searches for jelly in the waves.

~~~~~

The Calm

Snow-capped mountains,
barren, wind-whipped land,

photographs cold enough to raise chills.
Cigarette smoke reddens
the boy's eyes,
and he closes the magazine,
tucking the Sherpas back
into what might as well be fiction.
Stalls clean? the man asks.
Yessir, the boy says,
and he counts the bottles
beside the man's recliner.
The man nods at the magazine,
mutters, *Trash and lies*.
The boy's eyes settle on
the large hole in the wall,
recalls the night before,
a curse,
a scream,
a fistful of hair.
The man drinks,
lights another cigarette,
the boy straining with promises of a returning car,
palms wet on the cold, slick cover.

~~~~~

Suicide

The day you cracked your hand on the horse's skull,
I hid my mouth because I could not stop the grin.
And when your woman rose and cursed you even more
after you slapped her with all your strength,
leaving your lover's odor on her cheek,
and that night when the ashtray shattered the window
and the car door bruised her legs,
that night I fell into screams
which remain even now black holes in memory,
I swore I would never become you.

Eyes glare back from childhood mirrors;
the smell of your skin,
the heat of your temper, cling tightly.
Though I'll never admit to understanding

13

those nights, those screams,
all those times you could not deal,
I've made peace with the darkness.
Hypocrisy,
even in understanding,
has a way of killing.

~~~~~

Night Beats

His odor lingers in the room,
and his songs whine from the
record stack left on the stereo.
The gray edge of cigarettes
clings to the ceiling light,
and she shields her eyes
with a quivering hand.

The boy spears faces in the darkness,
smothering car beams that streak
gray moons through his window, across his wall.
He curls his knees to his chest
and, with eyes wide, dreams of leaving.

She wipes snot from her lip
and caresses the blue hand left on her face.
She is drifting when the boy peeks
around the corner, fingers thrumming thigh
to the beat of their nights.

~~~~~

Another Parental Death

In gray, wet cold,
she laughs, says
I should do well on the road,
being twelve with no money,
taking only the clothes I'm wearing
and no food, no way to get it
with nothing to offer.

I save my breath,
hang tough, and wait
for the moment
when I will possess
the meager requirements to leave.

A week later,
I am running anyway,
but with her instead of alone,
fleeing instead from him,
to hide for years in the house
of her sister and brother-in-law,
hearing true stories of terror
and infidelity, twisted by time.
She relishes seeing my face redden
with the mention of his name,
the color of my hate
fueling her own fire,
but when childhood rage
fades into midlife pleas
for a truce, for friendship,
she mutters daggers:

Had it not been for you,
I would not have left!

Then she snakes her arms out to me,
sniffling her love,
as if three words
and a few tears
are good enough for
resurrections.

~~~~~

Rocks

Spotters run the line,
troubleshooting,
accuse us with a glance:
rocks splay off trestle tracks,
splash into the river,

melt under rippled stares.

Now we ache to run from below railings,
to wave to the conductor
and engineer passing above,
scream, "Hello! Hello!"
Yet silent beside waters that
gnaw rot into creosote posts,
we fear they'll see beyond
our grins,
our waves of greeting,
and know us,
our rocks.

~~~~~

Smoke

Claims of champion blood
slide in through the open window,
striking through smoke
alongside the scent of manure.
The cowboy bellows laughter,
but the boy in the truck's darkness
hears only the *goddamns* of his father,
the constant gnaw at the set price.
He pictures his mother,
arms crossed in defiance,
rage in her eyes, backing her husband,
chewing, chewing, chewing.
The boy lifts the smoldering butt from the tray,
focuses on the fire, then turns it away,
drawing the wet end to his lips, pulling.
Smoke hazes his watery eyes,
borrowed smoke his mother will not define
as his own when she and her husband
curse each other over money spent
on dreams that fade with light.

The Accident

She told them:
He had to see for himself,
to make sure his daddy's okay.

I shivered in my pajamas,
breath breaking in ashen
jerks against the night.
Steam twisted up for the stars
off blood oozing onto the hood.

The old man babbled:
It happened too fast to stop—
I didn't even see him.
A bubble of air burst
from a battered nose,
spattering droplets of red.

We'd heard the thud,
then Mama slipped shoes onto my feet,
a coat around my shoulders.
Your daddy's fine, just fine.
I yawned and stumbled after her
along the dark trail to the roadside arena
where I mingled with nervous whispers
as she pushed in close.

I found him in the shadows, watching her.
He dropped an empty beer bottle
as she stared into milky eyes.
She winced, absently touching her bruised cheek.
Tears shimmered as her trembling fingers
stroked the horse's broken face.

~~~~~

Monroe

That year,
behind the horse stalls,
with rabbit weed streaking

the pasture in gray and black,
we stripped stalks bare,
took the county edition
and tore it to length,
laid in the leaves,
rolled it tight,
curled our tongues end to end,
spreading spit so the paper
would burn slowly,
wouldn't go up in flames,
struck the match to one end
and drew on the other,
fought the crush in our chests,
and wondered if Marilyn
had felt it, too, the day before,
her cherubic face curling,
singeing into ash
under our noses.

~~~~~

Parent Child

At a nickel a piece,
you slaved over the neighbors' clothes:
extra money for groceries,
the chicken and canned peas.
How I cherished the aroma of Piggly Wiggly
and hated dirt under my nails, that sign
of white trash, small rooms, and outhouses.

It was good training,
hard work, little pay.
Learned to do without
luxuries like phones
and voices that cared.
You trusted, and I trusted—
to a point.
Remember the blood that soaked my underwear?
My navel still itches,
even when I scratch off the skin.

Penny

Penny refused to enter the woods that day,
rearing gently, but not high enough to throw my balance.
Legs hugging her sides, I lay against her neck,
mane brushing my face,
petted, stroked, coaxed, but she would not enter
the place we'd entered countless times before.

She had gone everywhere with me, for me—
into thickets and brambles,
alongside the busiest highway,
into the river where I dove from her back.

He had yelled the night before
that I was worse than my mother—
this, after the woman told me about the pills,
the ones that assured her
no others like me
would surprise her or him.
So we rode away,
Penny and I,
but at the woods, she balked.
Then my mother's voice
called in the distance,
tinged with something more than frustration.

Penny reared once more,
settled, tucked her head,
and entered the brush,
and I rode.
I rode fast away from
those days,
those voices.

Becoming

Third Generation

His father's hands
have broken on the skulls of horses,
have sacrificed fingers
to misplaced freezers and reckless saws,
have swollen from endless days in fields
brown by lack of rain and experience.

The screwdriver trembles
in the young man's grasp
as profoundly as the cup
years ago in his grandfather's hands,
coffee spilling,
until the old man's palsy
steadied on memories
never revealed.

He wonders whether gentle thoughts
ever calm his father's hands,
the memory of flesh against flesh,
but his own hands, driven by purpose,
steady and powerful,
crave acknowledgement
once, just once.

~~~~~

Bass

Desert heat and stinging sand,
that's the world of our future,
so say most who lay bets on signs.
But I am a fisherman,
casting into a pond that boils
with trout centuries ago:
My father stands on house steps, calling,
"Boy, lightning's gonna strike you dead,"
but my line's taut in this thunderstorm,
and I lean into the struggle,
reeling against the fighter,
a mighty opponent,

yet he is mine, all five pounds,
raised high, a trophy
flopping against my forearm,
my fingers hooked into one gill.

Now, in late nights, with images dancing
on a screen where nothing is real,
I hear whispers of the signs
that warn the end is near,
the end is here—
mysteries that befuddle me.
All I know is that the pond
is smaller than it used to be
and the bass don't put up
as big a fight these days.

~~~~~

At 16

conscience is but
a wall forming
like breasts,
small,
firm,
under hand,
a breathless voice
whispering out of
backseat darkness:
Why is this
so important?

~~~~~

Familiarity

When it doesn't go quite your way, you withhold the words
I've come to expect at the end,
drawing them instead reluctantly from me.

Suckered again, I curse myself for taking my first breath;
I curse you for not taking precautions.

An hour later, you're so light, so cheerful, only hinting
at the pain I cause. And the words I expect at the end
come at the beginning, the middle and

the end:

a parrot

mouthing syllables
as cold and deadly as

bullets.

~~~~~

Celluloid

White light flashes
and a small motor whirs
behind a thick curtain
drawn at my request.
In the last pew,
I wonder when I'll
open the envelope
(having put this day
out of mind)
to find, instead of a letter,
living color in casket gray,
the stiff shell of
an aunt whose last image
had been breathless giggles
at some forgotten joke,
gentle hugs and pats
on the shoulder,
the laughing assurance,
she's tickled to death
I stopped by.

Fort Morgan

While they snored and filled the tent with gas,
I took the frying pan down to wash it
in bay water, wondering if sharks would swim close
enough to shore for me to stroke their jaws with
my fingertips. Sand scraped away the crust
of beans and bacon. I remembered how
Cory had grinned, saying something about
sleeping in a tent filled with boys.
We had watched the sulfur well bubble
water and fire until Jack, Rob, and Rick began
to nod from too much Bud and weed.

My parents taught me well, refusing me entry
to their room on dark nights, scolding me back
to bed where headlights arched across the wall
until, finally, sleep grew stronger than fear
of monsters lurking outside my window.
I used that at the shore,
closed my eyes and slid my legs into the surf,
taunting the jaws that might brave the shallows,
and made the sand my pillow. The sun slid up
from the bay and speckled iridescent shards
across my hands and the water in the pan.
One by one, the boys emerged from the tent,
asked me how long I'd been awake.
Cory said he wanted to go home.
I drove him the fifty miles back, the old Bug
lulling me toward the sleep that had escaped
me during the night. I don't know
if he wanted to touch me then, nor do I care.

Mom and Manuel slipped into the kitchen
from the trailer's back bedroom when I came in.
He stammered, said he was helping her
with the furniture, and I muttered I needed to lie down.
They could have howled like demon virgins,
and I would not have known the difference.

Part of Her

She left a spot of blood on the front seat
and laughed about it for months.
Part of me for you, she said;
then she kissed me quickly
and left me wanting more.

Clouds brooded over the beach as
a storm churned the gulf into froth.
The touch-football game ended
when lightning struck a dune.
The blood spot streaked as we huddled in the car,
the rain draining from our clothes to soak the seat.
She shivered against me, laughing, blushing.

Waves beat an easy rhythm on the night shore.
Her hair twisted in ghostly strands around her face
to caress me near.
When later she kissed me quickly
and slipped out of the car,
she smiled and wiped her eyes dry
before darkness flooded the space between us.

~~~~~

Sand

Recall how the sand
ground into our soles,
sockless in sneakers,
how we dropped KFC
beyond the reach of breaking waves
and waited for ghost crabs
to lurch out of their holes
to steal away the carcass?
We wondered whether they
picked the bones clean,
or if they broke and consumed
the dark remains as well.
Are crabs like dogs? you asked.
Will the bones compact in their colons?

26

We walked then, our jeans
soft and innocently moist,
feet sinking into gulf-soaked sand,
shards of luminescence exploding,
then fading around our footprints.
Back at the car, we sat
half-in, half-out, our shoes off
as we slapped sand from our toes,
that lingering grit of shielding dunes,
eating into our skin
through damp underwear.

~~~~~

Old Games

This damn video game winks out
for the last time.
I wander room to room,
staring through windows
at the old bone-thin woman
and the boy,
pitching a silver dollar
back and forth
at tiny holes
dug at their toes.

He giggles,
collides into her knees,
and my joystick
tumbles into the garbage.
Yellowed paper
peels back from silver,
withdrawn from a bureau drawer.
Hands tremble.

~~~~~

Tell Me

Through scratches and faded lines,
the story's evident.

There, on the fender of a state police cruiser,
you pose in your tight skirt,
trim hair and bobby socks,
but who's that faceless, hatted shadow
behind the wheel?
Was he the first argument?
Or just a rebuttal when it came to blows?

Skip ten years and the edges aren't so tattered.
Your eyes glitter in the K-Mart instant-shot:
no poses, no winks, no more
primping for the battle—
just a woman, a quarter, and four flashes.
Tell me…why the sad and bitter glare?
Where's that keen-eyed girl
who wore the anklet a year before the one
you still dream about came to fill
those difficult hours between egg and meat?
Where is the giggling grin?
And all that butt-shaking
for the boys cluttering the small-town square
while the world awaited?

~~~~~

Tiddlywinks with Satan

That week, she said
your name a lot. I wish
she could've seen you.

(And smelled the odor
in the teenager's hair
the day Uncle Beryl died,
saying, the boy's been smoking.
No, no. Well, yes,
but a tobacco that would
damn me a pagan sinner.)

I miss her pumpkin pies,
her smile from the recliner,
her open *Bible*.

She worshipped you.

(And praised Jesus
when the seven-year-old
got baptized, saying,
the boy'll be a preacher.
No, no. Well, yes,
but of flesh,
she would say, and surely
accuse me of playing
tiddlywinks with Satan.)

Daddy cusses me,
always cussed her.
She never asked for him,
only you.

(But slapped the five-year-old
for breaking the shed window,
saying understanding comes with time.
Yes, yes. Well, no,
and I wonder
had she not left blue marks,
would I have returned
for an earlier goodbye.)

~~~~~

at the point of too far

damn right
dreams are made
to replace responsibility
for nightmaring
others' sleep
ripping into lives
that know nothing of things
their daddies and mommies
did to my daddies and mommies
but let's saddle them anyway
some clown's got to pay
god are you listening

quit diddling in my life
unless you plan to make me rich
damn right
and give me food
and fancy clothes
and gold and silver
and cars as big as apartments
damn right
and let me tell you
one thing
god and country
i am
equal to the best
a lot better than the rest
damn right

~~~~~

My Father's House

Scarecrow fingers scratch at black clouds
and the turtle at the road's edge
draws into its shell as I stop,
hands on knees, gasping.
Distant thunder grumbles.
Pickup lights slice through predawn gray,
spotlighting me like a possum,
freezing me as still as twenty-nine years ago
in the thin beam of a flashlight,
urine sparkling out the open window,
my father's voice cursing me
for not braving the darkness to the outhouse.

The truck slows, gives wide berth,
the driver unused to people this early.
I set the turtle further into the ditch,
then turn back, my pace quickening
as sharp streaks of electricity crackle closer.
I am racing to the house of my father,
equipped with inside plumbing and another wife.
Later, he will laugh to his friends about his boy
who's in for the weekend, "first time in years,"

how the boy ran five miles in the storm
("Now ain't that the craziest thing?")
before the rest of the world
had even thought about facing the day.

Carnalities

Making Ants Pop

Attacking straight up,
a stock-and-trader of lies,
like lovers on a couch
for the first time.

(I rise on chopstick arms, drunk.
Harpooned some brain cells tonight.
Thought we'd have time, love,
for a quick toss and a nightcap.
You look like a corpse in this light,
your eyes glazed, your mouth wide.
Am I too morbid?)

Making a living the hard way,
a schemer of conscience,
like cheaters in the balcony
trying to quiet the baby.

(I scratch my eyes.
They burn with too many forgotten nights.
I'd scratch them out if I knew I wouldn't
fall down the steps and pull you with me.
You look like an actress in this light,
your lines misread, your cheeks wet.
Am I too critical?)

Claiming it's all good fun,
a carnival master of mistakes,
like kids with a magnifying glass
making ants pop.

~~~~~

A Question of Balance

The night screams hollow
with the roar of semis,
stars spiraling into
a jagged-tooth sky.
This light—

this spattering of space—
sends the dogs howling,
skin crawling,
as the ambulance shrieks
into a fetid night-wind.
Eyes glass,
bruises define,
questions badger, end:
You sure you didn't just
bring it on yourself?

And knotted in bed, we
drift through heat pump hums,
nursing rhymes into dreams
while the world goes mad.

~~~~~

Bruised

Bruises.
She craves
bruises—
here, she says,
fingertips
hesitating, drifting
across her breasts,
down her abdomen
to her inner thighs—
a garland of desire, of love
that will fade as certainly as
the petals of a summer rose.

~~~~~

One Last Caress

She is watching at the window
as I shed the lawn mower.
She holds a glass of iced tea
in one hand,
a paint brush

in the other—
a job in the bedroom
to be done
under the ether
of fresh-cut grass
sifting in on July's
southern breeze.

When at last today
I brush the final stroke
and shudder with fatigue,
she'll cup my hand against
her breast
for one thing more,
one last caress,
and remind me of what I must do
tomorrow.

~~~~~

Carmel

She has this *thing* for cripples,
even lives with a guy who can't walk,
who has to be hospitalized every couple
of months for therapy. She says
she sticks with Rick once a month
because she finds him interesting,
not like the rest of her former clients.
Rick says he called the service,
and she appeared on his doorstep
the first time in hardly anything
but fiery hair and high heels,
*and we've been swinging from
chandeliers ever since.*
She told me she doesn't like her father,
something to do with a neighbor
when she was a young girl, a guy
peeping into her window, snapping
pictures as she dressed. He buried
something under her house with her father
watching, but she never crawled under

to dig it out. This Christmas, she says,
she will, even if it kills her father.
She hasn't written to me in months,
and I hear through Rick that her flatmate's
back in the hospital. The last time we talked,
she was having problems at her job.
Someone had gone through her
glove compartment, had found her list
of former clients, the names
of the few she still services.
Doesn't matter, she said.
We're all clients to some.
And whores to others.

~~~~~

Currents Scattering

Forget the cats for now.
Listen to the water
running the roof's gullies,
the drip in the chimney.
It's a gray day and worth
pausing a moment.
Used to take time out
on days like this to
count hairs on my arm
or ants fleeing across the threshold,
seeking higher ground.
Now there are dishes, litter boxes,
clothes to be ironed for tomorrow.
And us. Let's not forget us.

Pieces of heaven used to splatter me,
but now, safe under this roof,
I search the street gutter river
for a sign from a Savior.
In time,
you might remind me if
we still believe in something.

The western sky is clearing,

and the sun sparkles through raindrops
dangling like stars from maple leaves.
I drift with your voice
like smoke into the sky,
dissipate on currents scattering,
and pray to surrender like rain.

~~~~~

Darts

He says:
I like the women here.
(The line crackles with static.)
They pretend to *worship*
American men like gods,
but I'm not fool enough
to believe they really do—
only what we give them:
rings, bracelets, nightclubs,
condominiums, convertibles.
Jesus, man, let me tell you
about *her*, the one I'm with.
She's unreal, like,
have you ever known a woman
who could shoot darts from
there and hit
you at ten feet?
I swear! She's all over me.
Imagine the possibilities.

I mutter: *What?*
And he says, Never mind.
I knew you wouldn't understand.

~~~~~

Living Room Fire

She surrounds the log in fire,
blue, flickering,
licking away the bark,

sparking outward, upward.
Sap drips;
wood sizzles,
crackles, splits.

Embers fade past two,
and tomorrow night she'll
brush ashes from the hearth,
remember
the slow-burning heat,
kindle another log,
wrap herself
in flames.

~~~~~

Fumble into Fancy

I hear her whisper
between the crackle,
rings of time ashing,
see her eyes flicker
among the flames.
With wine,
I drift, and she
consumes my loneliness:
she is
always here, somehow,
burning inside me.

Her touch is ghostly,
a sense of memory
coupled with expectation,
a future in the
making of a past.

Her flame engulfs me,
a flourish
of scorching flesh,
and I dance
on the breath of fire,
embers that fuel

my fumbles into fancy:
she is
always here, somehow,
believing in me.

~~~~~

The Oddest Moments

Your words
float into mind
at the oddest moments—
in the pasta aisle,
in the car at dusk,
in the library on cold mornings,
in the kitchen with dirty dishes—
as though you're whispering,
like that day
in the marsh grove
when promises were
as bold
as the blood
that reddened
our cheeks
under touches
that took our breath,
as exciting
and comforting
as lies.

~~~~~

In the End

These days the sun shines hotter,
and the sea, so they say, is rising.
Cars are faster, boys bolder, girls as well,
and we feed from rise to slumber.
Along the road, bodies blur past,
and I reach to take you, kiss you,
stranger,
the sky darkening in our embrace,

this moment inhaled,
taken deeply,
released,
forgotten in the call,
the endless quest to attain
with nothing to give
and no mind for loss.
Burn sun,
rise ocean,
rage on wind.
Close our eyes.
Kiss me.
Release.

~~~~~

Late-Night

Christie lies open
across her chest.
Down the hall,
the toilet gurgles—
monotonous as raindrops.

She turns, the novel
slips to the floor,
slaps shut.
She stirs gently,
settles in down.
And I peel back the sheet
and imagine her
the way she wishes.

In late-night,
the bed quivers,
the toilet drones,
blood rushes.

Monkey See

I'm standing in the back corner
when she sidles up to me,
forefinger extended from her glass,
nailing the memory,
her colors perfect, a smear of red
on the tumbler's edge,
shadows in her eyes,
lips pouting, mocking,
and she says:
I hear you write books now.
She says:
I remember our chemistry class,
and it wasn't writing
that interested you then.

I sip my drink, glare into the ice
beyond my nose, and remember
times that reunions are supposed
to make me remember:
always too much to drink or smoke
with too little dignity.
(The old cliché: me,
taking yes for no, slipping
fingers under the material,
grazing flesh against the palm.)

So why didn't we do it?
she asks, and I shrug,
as her eyes narrow,
the tumbler's rim poised
below her parted lips,
and I try to remember her odor,
the way she felt, the way I felt.
I shrug, say:
I don't know; scared, maybe.
And she snickers.

She is talking again,
her tone lighter as she
glances around the ballroom,

searching for someone,
wanting to point me out
the way she would point to
a chimpanzee at the city zoo.

~~~~~

Wasn't That a Party?

She is standing
in someone's shadow,
drink mislaid,
thinking about
the bus ride home.
He is babbling through
wet lips that spurt
lies as easily as
lemons make them pucker.
(I saw him brush her breasts,
but she is too shy to say
anything at all.
At all.)

I wither
in someone's shadow,
drink in hand,
thinking about
my last drive—home?
A frame of mind,
I hear *him* say,
his lips rippling, tripling.
(His hand slipped
into my pocket
and fondled my soul—
only for a moment;
had I not been drunk
with my eyes hung down,
I would have noticed
nothing at all.
At all.)

Quittin' Time

She had a way
of setting
wind on fire.

Gnarled hands quiver
as ravens gather
in trees out back.
There's a growl in the kid's
stomach, but he's hungrier
for the girl
across the street.

I'm not so old
I've forgotten.

The bell rings,
the pump gauge clicks
years off in gallons.
Hands tremble under
layers of grease
that leave traces
even when the skin
is scrubbed pink.

The nozzle hangs,
the cap screws tight,
the driver pays.

The girl across the street
ignites stars in the boy's eyes,
and I tell him to cut out early—
some extra time to scrape
against the layers of the day.

I brace against the register,
face streaked and red,
as a fiery wind kisses my lips,
whispers past my ear:
It's quittin' time.

Saturday

Three a.m. Saturday:
Any scream of mine would fade
into the grunts, the groans
of the weekend lovers
in the next apartment.

Heat stifles selectively,
and they pump moans till one
comes under the last touch:
Their silence smolders on
my lover's cotton sheets.

"What was the noise?" she asks
through parted, sleepy lips.
And I reply, "Heat strokes."
She is almost pretty
as she smiles, rolls, sleeps.

Four a.m. Saturday:
Beads of perspiration drip hard,
exploding on my pillow.
Our sheets are soaked with the
idle sweat of hot nights.

~~~~~

Sinking

Memory serves:
once wine was not a prerequisite.
It came as easily as the sweat
that clung to our pores,
our bodies stroking melodies
like bow on viola,
until we could
shudder no more.

In nights planned,
we numb ourselves,
pretend to be giddy,

burn our backs and knees
on the living-room rug,
sleep till ten,
rise cotton-mouthed,
a gnawing between our temples,
stare into mirrors
at lines around our eyes,
an epitaph.

~~~~~

Slow Fans

In burning nights,
I spread my hands
like slow fans
keeping flies off
old ladies on
Sunday morn.
Cool flesh ripples,
she sighs and slides
to the wall,
lights cigarettes,
streams epitaphs
on shadows.
I etch pictures
of old ladies
chewing mints
in time to slow
fans, hot sermons.
She wheezes
something about
excitement,
turns away: I
spread my hands like
slow fans, stroke
mortality,
feel it rise.

Debating the Problem of Simple Sores

I have a cold sore and wonder
if I should kiss you.

It took a week
for the damn thing to bubble up.
(I had hoped you'd stop reading
long enough to put your hands on me.
I waited in bedroom darkness
each night after you grew drowsy from words,
waited till your breaths were heavy, steady,
then rose to the kitchen
to caress
and soak a paper towel.)

Tonight, the books are closed:
you're interested
in my meager offerings—
a side-mouth kiss,
a brush against your breasts.
Your hands become
magic.

~~~~~

The Path

Under a canopy of
cedar, mimosa, pine, and oak,
she ran the path
until it spilled into a field of
daisies, daylilies, dandelions.
When he broke free of the trail,
the flowers had swallowed her,
betraying no crushed petal
nor broken bloom,
no sign at all.
Bees, dizzy with nectar,
swirled through the crystalline air,
and the flowers waved
in the breeze.

Under Sheets

Heat settles:
I writhe below
a dead air
conditioner
under sheets,
cursing you.
This new one
in me lies
as often
as you smiled.
Damn you.

Too hot for
this new one:
I wiggle toes,
stir a breeze
under sheets.
If the a-c
did its job,
I would not
remember
you at all.

~~~~~

This Woman

Consider this woman.

Drunk and numb, I rise
from her, take my place on
the patio, stare at
other buildings that surround us.
"Fuck you," someone screams,
and a door slams.
Sweat stings my eyes.
The air is thick,
and I ache for
something familiar, soothing.

She whispers what I want to hear,
draws me back inside,
and I lower myself into darkness,
a dream of what I'll never be.

Coupled

Words

Recall how he snapped the picture
the second day we knew each other?
Yearbook material, he said,
but we'd hidden our faces,
although the lens caught our eyes
peeking from behind fingers spread.
I glued the shot
on the empty page
still reserved for you.
My words splattered your book,
and again, years later,
another in celebration of rings.
I've been too free with words,
expecting the same. It's taken
several lifetimes to understand
that words flow as easily as blood,
then clot on pages and minds
as quietly as solar breezes or
as furiously as thunderstorms.
Nothing like a faded photograph.
Comes down to points of view, I suppose.
I wish I knew, my dearest.
I wish I knew.

~~~~~

Ashes

What will they remember?
That he loved some too much
and never said?

I saw the urn on the mantel.
A picture sat before it,
a ring, a watch.
He looked young, she said,
but he got old fast.
Didn't like crowds
or parties and said
he hated the world,

but she knew him,
knew the truth.
She loved him.
And she showed him.
That was enough.

~~~~~

Local Love

(originally titled The Dark Side)

"Two hours, they'll be kissing—
so lovey-dovey they won't even
remember." In the meantime,
blood streams down her face.

Twenty yards ahead,
a man raises his fist,
and the woman begs
then slumps under his blow.

Four runners change their routes.
"Hey, man, you're hurting her."
"This ain't nothing to you—only me."
The woman struggles.

Joggers speed their pace away;
service-station hands turn backs.
"Big man, hit a woman. Come on,
come—" A wild swing, ripped shirt,

and still he has her when the
police arrive. "She threw my
things out my bag. *My* bag.
What can I do? Then he comes up,

acts like it's his business.
Call me names." And the cop
turns me aside, says it's just
another part of paradise.

"Like aloha, right?"

The cop blushes.
"Let me tell you
about local love."

~~~~~

Catch Phrase

At what point did change occur?
And exactly what has changed?
Crumbs on the table,
clothes on the washroom floor:
Our sheets now smell of sweat,
sex's crimson odor
bleached months ago.
Voices scream second guesses,
and, somewhere in there,
you sigh, and I realize
what you must already know,
but "working through" has always been
the catch phrase here.
Dishes in the sink,
dust in corners,
your hair spread upon the comforter:
Your eyes dance in dreams.
I kiss your cheek,
whisper goodbye/hello.

~~~~~

Crow

circling.

Sweat blinds.

She whispered to him this morning,
What's your day?
A shrug of shoulders.
Mine, too.
He swept away the morning's dishes,
watched her drive off for work.

In the back of his mind,
those years,
all those years.
Tears and laughter.

Breath pumps the chest.
Old bones, fatigued muscles,
running, day after day.

Sweat blinds.

Circling,
crow.

~~~~~

Afterbirth

I am tired of hangers on doorknobs,
of milk dried in bottoms of cups,
of magazines on the kitchen table,
of vacuuming carpets,
of clothes in closet hampers,
of oil draining from cold engines,
of whims,
of *dramadies*,
of hormones,
of speaking quietly in the morning,
of saying I'm sorry,
of being forgiven.

I am tired.

You pat my knee,
tell me the house looks good,
car too,
kiss my cheek,
fall asleep on the couch.
Through the window,
I see the grass is high,
and a load of clothes
sours in the washer.

Diamond
—For Bonnie

Her breaths rustle
against the pillow
and I count them
millions into millions
of seconds I have lain
beside her in darkness
and savored
the odor of skin
that binds
past and future
into present
a silence
of knowing
it is right it is right.

~~~~~

Mother's Lover

They threw dirt in
Mother's lover's face
yesterday:
she discovered the obituary
three hours
after he was covered.

His heart—bloated,
overworked, a battered toy.
(I won't chain you to a dead man.)

The affair
endured Mother's temper
a decade.
(Fifteen minutes rapping on her door,
finally opening,
a red face peering over her shoulder,
smiling nevertheless:
warm hand,
soft voice.)

Wife, daughter,
responsibilities to
satisfy,
then on with a new life—
so the dream went.

Employment problems,
insurance adjustments, chest pains.
(You can't marry a corpse.)

She didn't stop
the last day she saw his truck
parked at the coffee shop
where they met to talk:
She was late.
She asks me how can she
deal with coffee breaks
in years to come.
At the coffee shop two days later,
the wife begins to teach her.

~~~~~

Encounters

She smiles to tell the truth,
but he pipes in, says,
We met in a bar.
I was turning tricks
and she wandered in.
She blushes behind laughter,
but he wonders how long
it will take until
she grows weary of such levity
and peers through the jokes,
piercing the sorrow, the desire beyond
what should be and what has been.

She taps her foot against his,
rolls rich brown eyes

toward his faltering smile,
and he brightens with a sigh.
That was the last night I did bars...
Their friend winks, chuckles,
You're a devil.

~~~~~

Enough

She says:
I'm in the time of life that's got me screwed.
I love him, god knows, but I have this capacity
to love so many others.
I don't touch, won't touch,
but it would be nice...
I want to spend my life with him.
It's just, it's just—
Damn it. I'm alive, one shot.
She says:
This is all I've got.

~~~~~

Accounting
   (originally entitled "History")

On these mornings when snow
floats on air like fireflies in spring
and sunshine sparkles in icy tendrils,
whatever else is happening fades,
and I imagine myself riding
those magic carpets of ice
into blue and silent peace.
They drift away, and I'm left again
to battle what I do not understand,
this passage...or is it destiny?
Self-fulfilling prophecy?

More love exists between us
than most, no doubt about that.
Hold me. Remember when

beach wind sprayed sand against our thighs
and we imagined all the beautiful things
the future held for us?
We had more words than history then,
whispers of children,
filled with hope and promises.

The last snow settles,
silence descending.
In glassy crystals, a sparkle,
shards of light, spilling, warming.

~~~~~

Kiss Me Onward

I have fallen,
I fear,
far too far
for even you to catch me.
One hundred percent
fatal,
such as it is,
under mists
I stumbled.

(You smiled every time
I made you cry.
I wondered then,
wonder now
why you even said
"yes,"
why you hold me the few
times I am tall,
catch me the many
times I fall.)

And still I ask you
to take me again,
kiss me
onward to the other side
for it is

barren,
freezing
even now
as I stumble and
slip between
the cracks,
years before
the end.

~~~~~

Mortality

My face was wet
with her tears tonight:
she was imagining.

A TV movie,
mindless acting,
laughable lines:

the husband lay dying.
He closed his eyes;
she pulled me close,
called herself silly.

I was imagining:
her face was wet
with my tears tonight.

~~~~~

Seconds

I'm a few days into a new life.
You can say this about the old one:
His marriage was better than most,
better than some.
Carve that on the tombstone.
Also, don't forget the trinkets
sold from that life's work.
Scratch them as postscript.

Now a new life, marked
by a fresh resident,
dependent as an invalid,
but getting better.
My friend is asleep in bed.
Two decades, we made that bed live,
made it rock and roll, baby.
Now the one who sleeps between us
cuts the mattress into thirds.

This new life frightens me,
I admit that much.
Traveling blind here.
Dependent keeps popping up,
and I don't like it applied to me.
Had forgotten youth,
singularity,
being alone.

And now?
Must reconsider routine
and joining and separation.
Man, boy, untethered,
stepping lightly into *secondhood*,
wary of the chisel.

~~~~~

One Thought

At some point,
someone will say,
bamboo,
and that autumn's heat
will come back to you
as intense as a vision,
how you pulled the culm
as I sank the spade under roots
and precious sprouts for transplanting,
how sweat shimmered on our faces
and stained our shirts,

how silence settled in the grove
as the salt of our skin
burned our tongues,
how much,
how truly much
I loved you.

~~~~~

A Quarter Invested
—For Paul & Dianne

A certain glance,
a roll of shoulders,
signals read by two as one.
Time, the smith of souls,
has fashioned a house of silver,
buttressed by foundations absolute:
respect, commitment, passion.
Two pillars, one roof.
Sanctuary. Home.

~~~~~

Old Reliable

It comes an hour before shift's end.
Two weeks, it has sat on a desk somewhere,
racing toward deadline, going nowhere.
We need this by Monday. Hope you didn't
have plans for the weekend.
(As a matter of fact...)

I know, but you understand how important it is.
And I'll be thinking about you, really;
hey, I'd be here if I could,
but I've got this family thing I can't get out of.
You understand.
(As a matter of fact...)
Glad we have someone as reliable as you.
Wish I could've looked over
the first draft before now,

but you know, with everything else—
hell, you understand.
(As a matter of fact...)

I know, but we need it first thing Monday.
You're lucky to have the kind of family you do.
Be glad you're not stuck with my wife and kids.
Do this, do that, go there, come here.

As a matter of fact, he says,
slouching around from behind the desk.
Then he sighs, Never mind.

A slap on the back: Monday then.

As he gulps from the hall fountain,
he wonders why people fear drowning,
and he tries to imagine his wife's face
when he'll phone her later, before she dresses,
to explain away one more Friday night.

~~~~~

Setting, Rising

Silver vases and wooden roses:
a life of memories, she says;
time now to reflect.
The sun has set, he says,
and so much remains to be done,
but moonbeams have slipped in
between the window slats.
What? she says,
but he's already moved on.

~~~~~

Private Tables

With soft voices
over steaming tea,
poems are made

then laid aside
in pieces:
We strive to form
face into word,
feeling into rhyme.

Meter mocks rhyme
that fails to make
life poems.
So we sip
at the steam
rising from our cups:

Another hand must grant
this life a poem,
inked from the trinkets
left behind:
empty cups in
cold rooms of
private tables.

~~~~~

Take My Hand, Take My Hand
—For Bonnie

They bend and twist in bursts of color,
limbs intertwined,
blanketing us with red and gold.
(And you whisper that someone will see,
but we are hidden
as always.
Take my hand, take my hand.)

They die with majesty:
Pompous,
mocking,
these peacock giants
who have shaded us
forever.
(As the wind strips them bare, you whisper,
someone will see.

So let it be—this moment:
Take my hand; take my hand.)

I will remember.
Always.

My leaves will blaze in colors
as I begin to wither.
(Take my hand, take my hand.)
I will bare my bones
to mount winter's winds,
the memory of your hand
still warm in mine,
still warm in mine.

~~~~~

The Beat

The beat, distant and constant
through the moonlight,
drives her to the window.
The neighbors again, she whispers,
but he doesn't hear her,
asleep in his chair.
She rests her forehead
against the cool glass
eyes toward the house
where light bleeds
through open shades
into the yard.
The day the couple moved in—
the man with dirty hands and tangled hair,
the woman, pregnant as the moon—
they had laughed as they climbed the stairs,
pausing to catch her watching.
The girl waved, and she smiled,
ducked back inside.
Their music began that night, the beat,
that steady thump, stroking her
in the dark room where she'd lain.
She touches her husband's wrist.

He stirs, settles.
She swims through waves of moonlight
to bed, her heart in time
with that other house.

~~~~~

Becoming

He whispers love
and steals her from innocence:
She is a feather
floating, tossing, dancing
through mists of becoming.
He rolls away and speaks
of how it should be.

Tap water strangles plastic pipes,
as pale light stabs through the doorway,
slicing the room in half.
And she shivers
on bare sheets,
curls into a metallic moon,
draping herself in nakedness.

Fingertips stroke eyelids,
brush cheeks in soft day-glow,
and she sighs as quietly
as jasmine drifting
like dust that flickers
in a room slivered by sunlight.
She draws her legs under words
that bear her away.

I caress her whispers
like a roof under raindrops,
bathe my face in her tears.
On this side of the hill
that she must scale alone,
I am helpless to still
the pain that sets itself in time
as firmly as footprints in stone.

In what dimension do memories await rebirth and rebirth and rebirth?

When I say I've never felt this way,
yet feel it all again,
that I'm seeking it out once more,
you smile, and tell me you understand,
even when you do not.
Eastward rolling storm,
the drone of rain on tin and leaves,
the scent of cherries and ozone—
such is the genesis of recognition,
that nagging, rooted desire to caress
a place, a life,
as ancient as they are new and luscious,
the barter of this soul of copper
for a soul of gold or flesh.
And still, somehow, I know that,
even when the feeling's gone,
I will have what I had all along:
home.

Relativity

Air

Blow my soul down
a culm half as long as my arm,
and Unk is waiting at the end,
seated with hands behind his head,
legs stretched, ankles crossed,
grinning around that old cigar.
He sailed past jungles
of *madake*, bullets whispering,
but that was a lifetime ago,
a life ago.

Smoke rises in one giant puff
from that misty grinning mug.
My air runs its course through
sound and sound and sound again.
His image fades,
bamboo moist
against my lips,
its song, its song
the voice of the dead,
rejoicing.

~~~~~

If Only A Moment

On a whim, he snaps
a stem from her
untended bed of roses,
careful not to prick his finger.
He climbs toward game show voices
screaming through the tattered screen door—
needs fixing, he thinks, but doubts
he will soon find the time.

He slips inside, calls
granny, granny,
and the TV falls silent.
Honey, baby, is that…?
A shadow, she appears

from the den, eyes clouded
with heavy lenses.
See what I've brought you?

She edges close,
quivering fingers
wrapping around the stem,
drawing the bud gently near her face.
How beautiful, she whispers.
A single bead of blood
shimmers on a thorn against her palm,
cries a thin path across
her pale, wrinkled wrist.

~~~~~

Business

Today, a land deal.

"They got two—special
price: eighty-nine down,
eighty bucks a month,
and interest free."

"No thanks, Mom. An urn's
fine." That quiets her.
She's fifty in two weeks;
two months, I'm thirty.

She said she grew up
twenty years ago:
Time to stop playing,
start paying.
I intend to play
a little longer.

At forty, she fell
apart, so she says—
made the doctor rich.

Now, she puts one foot

in the grave and insists
I join her in this package deal.
Her birthdays mean more than mine,
are always strictly business.

~~~~~

At 30

He picks his words carefully:
"I thought it would get easier."
And everyone laughs.

The cake blazes before him
and the child he lifts to help
blow out the candles giggles
and calls him an "old man."
His mother mumbles something
about Bessie to her brother and sister,
and their eyes blank, mouths twitch.

"You shouldn't live so far away,"
she says to him. "You're my son."
And he recalls endless explanations
uttered before at the terminal.
"When Bessie needed me, I wasn't there."
He shudders as her tears form again.

"I thought it would get easier," he says,
and he manages a smile, this old man.

~~~~~

Brother and Sister

He can leave anytime, she says.
Nurse told me.
The miles slide away under hot tires.
She recalls how he sat in the corner of the room
when the judge showed her where to sign.
If you don't, the judge said, I'll have no choice.
Her knuckles are yellow pale against the wheel.

The parking lot is empty at midweek,
the time she prefers.

Concealed in a Hardee's booth, our coffees
steaming, he stares northward out the window.
You remember...? he says to me,
and I feel her glare.
The coffee...
When you was a young boy and
you used to get me to put a quarter
in the jukebox to play that love potion song?

The coffees cloud.

When you gonna leave? she says.
They say you can go now.
He looks out the window, mutters,
Where?
You'll move in with me, she says.
Her hand fishes a calculator from her purse.
How much does the government give you a month?

~~~~~

Buzzard

Not much different from
vultures at the carcass:
Turn your back for a second,
and one will readily deliver
the decisive peck
to speed along the inevitable.

They talked about the funeral at his bedside,
about how he got fat
and then lost it,
about his wife,
about how he was part to blame for her early grave.
They blathered with the nurse
about the code down the hall
and wondered aloud
how in the world could a doctor expect

good nurses like her to save someone *that* old,
that far gone.

He lay there, eyes alive,
mouth paralyzed in silence,
hand trembling in mine,
aware, I am sure, I am sure,
the buzzards had landed.

~~~~~

Counting Change

She pulls it in around her,
copper *tinking* nickel,
clinking silver, scuffing gold,
and claims to him,
It isn't all here.
Buffalo, Indian,
Mercury, and Liberty
glare at her as she counts
two-by-two-by-two,
growling that her pictures
went missing like other coins,
after the bastard moved out,
after the divorce, the end—
pictures of the father,
the mother, the baby, the dead.

He wonders who he resembles more
as he fondles the wallet
that holds the single school shot
he escaped with twenty years ago.

~~~~~

The Bayou at Your Back Door

The lot sits on the bayou with
catfish sucking at the bank
in search of a sinker, a worm, a hook.
"You can't tell me you wouldn't

like to live in a place like this."
Pine needles rattle a symphony
as winter settles in the underbrush.
Ice waters lap tears against the bank.
"You'd love the bayou at your back door
and trees crowding the front yard.
And I'd be close if anything..."

A bluegill shatters the surface;
ripples spread in a circle, widening,
widening, until nothing remains
but a glassy mirror reflecting winter.
A squirrel edges from cover,
then pauses, sniffing for danger.
It bends, sips the bayou. A twig
cracks; the squirrel darts into
brown underbrush, shoots up a pine,
and quivers behind thorny cones.

The sun slides behind steel-gray,
and ice winds glide across the water,
piercing flesh, their voices
tasting, tempting, murmuring,
"The season's here."

~~~~~

Bottom of the Glass

With three coolers swirling,
it's easier
to deal
with simple things like
families,
funerals,
mirrors.

(The sun has set
on my doorstep
four times,
and not once have I been
burned—

look at my fingertips
if you doubt me.
Maybe this rain has
something to do with
my luck.)

You can't say I'm a drunk
just because it's
easier,
quicker,
looser
for me this way—
a bit more
laughter,
a few more
tears.

(I would sing for you
an opera
if I could hum even a song,
but on an empty stomach,
three coolers
and a few too many memories,
I wouldn't dare mutter
even my own name.)

Birds squawk
and shelter themselves under
dripping eaves
as rain pummels cracked,
dry clay into mud.

~~~~~

To Give a Child Choice

They ran lanes under me
that led nowhere I chose to go.
So I encased myself in walls,
which, in gloom and joy, caressed,
pretending nothing.

They hammered words into me
that painted dreams I never dreamt.
So I wrapped myself in my dictionary,
which, in desire and loss,
kindled my fire.

And for all they've tried,
they will never understand what they've done.

~~~~~

Father's Day

The third and last card
on my first gift shop day as "Dad"
arrived late, on the Wednesday following.
Of course, I'd done my duties,
remembered my own father
with cynical lines mailed on time,
but I've never believed in that Sunday.

What of my daughter?
Will she choose the single day
to speak through Hallmark?
It comes down to role, doesn't it?
Titles and deeds and time.
Tests passed or ignored.

Please give the day
to those who need it,
who require token thanks.
Toss the candy aside
and burn the cards.
Rewards earned are never so fleeting.

~~~~~

The Iron Bed

The iron bed rusted
a decade in the garage.
When she glimpsed the springs,

she saw her mother
thrashing against life.
Her nephew once asked to buy the bed,
to refinish and use in his home,
but she refused without reason.

Two days ago, Goodwill
hauled the bed away,
leaving four orange spots
in the concrete floor,
drawing her eyes each time
the garage door slides open.

~~~~~

Last Rite
—for Mo

Tell them to bury you at the edge;
I can't deal with obstacles when
the wine swims through my eyes.
Have them bury you with an ear up
so you can better hear
my twisted tongue effects
on the Greenhouse,
Disarmament, and
(our favorite) Family.

If I go first, don't let them
smother me with dirt;
instead, roast me into ashes
and set my cup at your table
where I learned to take,
to give, and to share.
And when you make love to JD,
spike your glass with
a sprinkling of me,
and I'll spin your mind
with madness one more time.

Machine

—For Arlene

Mechanical screening today,
and I've listened twice as you've demanded,
"Where are you? I don't like machines."
Funny how we've shaped our lives.
Take these machines you loathe:
I respect their indifference.
And when some internal mechanism fails,
the new, improved version is ready in the wings.

Remember my days searching
through clouds of Maui haze,
this redneck turned city boy?
I'd blow clouds through my bedroom window screen
while reading Carver by Bic lighter
with Anderson on the headphones,
weary of reliving your battered, bruised years.
I was there too, you know.

Then came the bout with Jesus,
but that wasn't right either,
not quite the Baptist way,
those hippies who mumbled ungodly gibberish
that could only mean drugs. Had that been,
I may have spilled the truth then.

Through Saturday nights and thin trailer walls,
the Mexican moaned about the bitch at home,
then he'd let you soothe his pain
while he promised to coax magic
from my old Decca guitar.
He always delivered.

Green light flashes, and even before
the message tape lurches, I know
the voice will be yours, speaking
to the only one who listens
without judgment, without decree,
absolute and businesslike—
less than human, more than humane.

The March

Whispers up the aisle:
The boy's one of the grandkids.
Twenty years ago, he had hair near 'bout to his butt.

The old man didn't care for the boy's hair,
but he respected the boy because the boy listened.
He didn't patronize the boy like the others.
And when the old man's wife died fifteen years ago,
it was the boy he chose to hear his regrets, his memories,
his gripes about the preacher who talked on and on
about Jesus instead of the woman who had touched
so many lives in so many ways.

Somewhere in the sweltering parking lot,
the relatives are lining up.
The boy starts for the exit to join them,
eyes diverted from the wrinkled faces
that accuse him of not viewing long enough,
but he prefers the image in his mind—
arms flailing in mock surprise
as a camera's shutter sounds,
freezing the old man under the peach tree
planted the year the boy was born.

The boy meets the family at the door,
and his father motions
for him to fall in with the march.
Halfway up the aisle, he realizes he should
be in back with the other grandchildren.
He stops, confused, seats himself in the wrong pew,
and his face burns as cousins smirk,
mocking with their eyes.
As the preacher spits heaven and hell,
the boy grins.
He glances around at the solemn, weathered faces,
and nods satisfaction, certain he's given
the old man reason to chuckle.

Mattresses

Are you lying on a mattress too soft,
wondering why the words are always harsh?
Or has the anger become the norm for you?

I wedge myself between clean sheets
on firm bedding and listen to the sleep
of a woman whose whispers warm like vapor.

What are you thinking now?
Are you dreaming of lovers past and son gone,
of gentle nights on back porch swings,
of sipping Coke and watching shooting stars
as your mind weaves a future sparkling?
Or are you lying with eyes open
in a dark bedroom
where memories haunt
and accusations ricochet between walls
like misaimed bullets?

~~~~~

Seeking Middle Ground

(If I could drink myself numb,
it would not sting so much;
but there's never enough wine.)
The sky is blacker than I've
seen it in years, stuck
here with you, listening
to you walk away again,
fresh tears rippling down cheeks
wrinkled by years of tears.
I'm waiting you out this time.
I'm not running in anger.
I'm not cursing myself.
I'm trying to explain:
I'm tired, I am tired,
ready to call a truce,
ready for us to be friends.
And you say you're so ashamed,

so ashamed for what happened
after the divorce,
so ashamed about the men who followed.
I say at least they were kind
and didn't beat their failures
into you with their fists.
But you swear you'd be with *him* now,
had it not been for
the eleven-year-old, me, you say
you would have stayed,
no matter what.

~~~~~

Your Funeral

—For Mo…again

Last night, I dreamed you died.
A glorious funeral,
with hundreds packing the chapel
in the middle of the cemetery
near the plots where your parents lie.
The same preacher who stumbled
over your father's life
mispronounced your name
and blinked in the silence
of us who knew you.
Your crippled son and second husband
filled the row of pity
as your first husband
watched from the rear where rain
brushed against the outer doors,
diminishing my steps up the aisle.
I held the podium, scanned faces
I have seen you among all my life:
Your brother in his beer stained stillness;
his wife, her sunken, distant eyes;
their daughter, face hidden by clouds;
your friends, muddled or sleeping—
all once rescued by your grace,
your time, your money,
now lost, so lost.

I have no tally-sheet for souls, I said,
no scorecard for Jesus,
only memories of a savior,
a Mary in the dark times when
parents were fists and death a prayer.

Years ago, you faded
into marriage.
It was in the pale smoke
of oak leaves on gray autumn air
I found you drifting between roles.
That's when I knew you.
That's when I loved you.

~~~~~

Waiting for the Old Man

In the bedroom, the sister sorts through
long-sleeve shirts (all he's ever worn)
then folds two into a suitcase,
its leather sides matted
with cobwebs from the First World War.
Her brother touches her shoulder,
and she turns to his chest, sobbing,
it's the unexpected moments,
a bike or pocket watch...
And what are we going to do about the TV,
his wardrobe, the rickety bed?
Remember the seventy-pound watermelon
that summer of '62, and Mama—
remember how he got when she died?

It's the unexpected moments, she sniffs again,
turning away, snapping the case shut.
She's ready, she says, for the hospital.
By late afternoon, she'll be at the nursing home,
repeating to the staff,
it's for the old man, only for him.

Recycling

Let's be cool tomorrow,
my cousin says to me;
no arguments, you understand?

He fingers the beer can before him,
then stacks it with other empties
(six I count). He pops
the top on another from
the paper bag at his feet.
Says he saves the cans
for recycling:
hell, it just makes sense,
what they're doing to the
earth and all, and I ask
him about glass bottles;
says it doesn't pay enough.

I ask about his sister;
says she ain't talking to him,
says she can't appreciate
the fact he doesn't do death.
Who needs a bunch of bastards
telling him how sorry
they are for his loss
and how hard it's hit his father?

I don't do death, he repeats.
He's worn a track
around the backyard perimeter,
drinking, walking, drinking.
On the patio's another bag
filled with empties,
ready for the recycler.

I say, I need to check
on my mother.
He says, keep it cool tomorrow,
you hear? No problems.
No arguments.

He walks the path,
another can at his lips,
a stumble to one side.

~~~~~

Screening

Phone's rung three times a day
for months with no voice
to say who's calling or why.
He hears background noise,
like bar chatter or a TV,
but it's so negligible
the machine disengages
before the caller hangs up.
His wife is on the job,
on the road, when the calls come.
His relatives live far away.
Some are old.
The phone rings.
His fingertips tremble
against the receiver.

~~~~~

Last Rite Revisited
—For Mo, 10 years later

We renewed over burning leaves,
piles you and your first husband
had raked between shouts at your son,
Get back, stay back.
Smoke rose for days,
and, before the last embers succumbed,
you were back in the house next to your parents',
sipping whiskey with your dad,
cursing your mother for meddling
and entering through the backdoor without knocking.

Your shined kitchen table supported coffee, tea, liquor, wine,
and bore the weight of our laughter and tears.

Freedom reckoned well with you and those who gathered there.
As fires smoldered, you smiled at your son's curses against his father—
a part of you stripped away, a judgment discarded—
and chuckled when I said Buddhism's a pretty good idea.
We drank with your father until that next man came,
until the table began to sustain lighter loads,
until time and views wedged between us,
until your father left for good.

We recalled your father's life in the same sterile room,
seated far from each other, inches away.
Lightning crackled through the preacher's sermon,
but, if he saved any souls at the expense of your dad's life,
I saw none take his hand.
You greeted within the skin of your new man,
and I noticed how thin you'd become,
despite the weight you'd gained.
In the end, you glanced at the preacher
retreating, asked if I was still an atheist.

We made a pact years and years ago,
but, as you say, times change—souls, too.
Still, when I'm gone, when I am ashes,
pause one last time to sip whiskey
sprinkled with madness.
Recall us at that table, sharing secrets,
fresh with the essence of fire in our hair,
embers still glowing upon the ground.

~~~~~

Severed

No regrets,
she bragged after he died.
I do what I want and to hell with everyone else.
Father and daughter in their silence, eternal,
well beyond the grave.

And now it comes to turns and terms,
when wishes aren't what daughter
had in mind, but are prime

to draw the circular glare,
trumping the sympathy play
as she hurls silence
at the next generation.

No thanks.

She settles in her chair,
in her room,
television blaring,
and sucks Godivas,
recalling when less
scripted voices
filled this house.

~~~~~

Stats

He bought me off
with four hundred at Christmas,
two in April
and a card that read how
wonderful a boy am I.

Twenty years I cursed him,
and now the decades
have backed him into a corner.
The end of another marriage
has put him alone again,
a statistic.

Stats lie,
buy, cry.
And die.

So do fathers.

And sons.

The First Stroke

He is silent,
slouched over the wheel,
truck idling,
when his son finds him.
"Finally," the son
mutters, then opens
the door and frowns.

"The doctor said
he'd be okay,
but it might
affect his mind."

He thanks his son
for everything,
from dinner to dishes,
and the son is glad he lived.

"Those first days,
he was as humble
as a person can be.
Then last night
he said he's gonna stick
a gun to my head.
I remember Mama,
then look at him
and wonder why it couldn't
have been different."

The floor creaks in another room,
and the son's eyes redden.
He starts for the door,
pausing to call back,
"Phone if you want me
to bring you dinner."

The Second Stroke

Tobacco stains the front of his shirt,
mis-*spit*,
like his youth, he'd say,
if he still made jokes.
"I ain't no 'count,
just no 'count."
His eyes, time-faded gray,
muddle and drift.
"He was rough.
Marked her up for weeks.
You don't remember that, do you?
He helps 'round here now,
but he was…"

Rough, cracked vinyl creaks like pine
under shifting bones;
the Folgers can between his legs
reeks of Skoal.
He swipes his lips with
the back of a quivering hand.

"Everything went to hell—
course you know what I mean.
I tried to help them.
But he…
He helps out here.
Your mama okay now?
He was rough."

Two weeks ago,
he would have used a .38
had the door not been locked
from the other side.

"I ain't no 'count now,
but I used to be.
I used to be."
His eyes close;
black spittle dribbles off his chin.

The Third Stroke

"You treat each other right,
and…" Words escape.

Winter settles in his room
like an August dog day.
Propane fire whispers,
yet he shivers, tobacco breath
curling around his eyes,
streaking shadows.
"I try to keep busy,"
mutters this man who howled in
his first breath ten years
after his daddy's slaves
headed north.

The cigarette dies between
trembling fingers
and he stares into faded portraits
as if they were newsreels.
His lips form "Naomi"
to the withered images,
but his voice hisses
for another smoke.

He realizes
he's not alone.
"You cold?"
then his eyes wander,
and words muddle
through mistakes and time.
He pulls a cigarette from the pack.
The match quivers
between tobacco and photographs.

"You treat each other right,
and…" Words escape.

And the Wife

He's been talking about fishing all month,
anticipating my visit, the first in two years.
Father and son in a boat, on the river,
casting with more than bait and hooks.
He's at the door, staring out, hands on his hips,
shaking his head at the drizzle that's been falling
since my arrival two days ago, time I've spent sitting
in this office as he hawks used cars.
He shakes his head again and turns back,
lighting a Camel, adding smoke to already stale air.
Guess we could go anyway, he says,
but the wife from behind the counter says,
And do what, honey, catch pneumonia?
Can you stay a couple of days more? he says to me,
but the wife, coming around now, says,
That'd be all right, honey, if he wants to,
but he'd have to go with you to the car sale,
and I don't think he wants to stand around
all day, just watching you buy cars.
He shrugs and sits at the negotiating table
where I drift toward the time I can say
I need to get back to work, that I'll come again.
He will accept my words as I will accept his promise
to visit me four hundred miles away, soon, real soon.
We watch the river of rain together in silence,
him, holding the Camel loosely between his lips,
me, breathing in his tired, smoky exhalations:
father and son.
And the wife.

~~~~~

Thomas

That metal putter
and the wooden drivers
made more of a mark for him
than the decades at Monsanto.
He cried for the past
two years: Doctors said

his wife would be dead
by now. Hacking blood
and wheezing, she fooled them.
They've poked and prodded, he said,
until she no longer cares
who sees her tits sag.
He spent two years of retirement
at home, playing granddad to
the adopted daughter's brood,
tending his wife,
and crafting clubs
that send balls straight
down the fairway. He
told everyone how much
he loved her, how much
he already missed her.
I still picture him
at the last reunion,
winded but grinning,
in red shorts,
white socks, black loafers,
clenching, stretching
his left hand, wishing
he was on the green.

~~~~~

Time Rings

He sits behind
a half-century of wrinkles
softened by smoke
hovering like a ghost above
the desk. He mumbles,
If I ever get like him,
put me away—put me away
and forget me.
He answers the phone
with a snatch of the receiver,
a snatch in his voice.
Lines deepen:
They'll take him this weekend?

He stares out a blank window
and softly wheezes in the
smoke that twists up from
the ashtray. He mutters,
With the old man gone...
And he shakes his head, drifts.

His wife cocks open the door,
says the lawyer will
see them in an hour.
A creak of hinges closing:
Too many things at once.
He slips the ring from his finger,
lets it plink onto the desktop,
manages a solemn smile.

A week from now, he says,
I'll have no one to bother me.

~~~~~

Unk

What would he think about these flutes,
these pieces of bamboo, whispering
melodies that could make chill bumps
crawl on the skin of any man who survived
Kamikazes?
On his ship, he saw the plane
explode across the deck,
buddies blown overboard in flames,
scattered in pieces, splattering, splattering.

This flute breathes, sets sail, and I can almost believe
that music is stronger than hate, stronger than life itself,
and I hear him say, *Play something sweet, young buck.*
A real sweet song.

Worms

When I number the dead,
I come up with no more than one,
saving all others for
more opportune times.
The ragged halls
are drenched in golden mist
as cool air whispers in.
I am comfy in my down wrap,
my feet are warm,
and I remember Eber's worms.

He dreamed of wiggling red worms
in an earthen bed,
churning, procreating,
a promise of riches.
I climbed the state tower with him
a thousand times to stretch
my eye down a spotting scope
to points where smoke rose
from careless camp fires
or fires ignited by smoldering cigarettes
(like those that nailed his lungs together),
and he would say, someday, my boy,
worms, my worms…

In the evenings, he raked the worm bed,
spoke of grand plans for us all,
but when smoke finally forced him
to lay his rakes aside,
he found that he'd only worked himself
into potting soil.

~~~~~

Driving with James

He was crazy even back then,
setting the boy in his lap
when the boy's feet couldn't
touch the pedals from the seat,

chancing lives on the boy's
ability to keep the wheels
steady, right of the yellow line.

Fear flickered in the eyes
of drivers unaware
of the guarding hand,
but that was before the voices came
and told him to trust no one,
especially the eight-year-old boy
with death at his whim.
When the voices deserted him
in that white shoe place,
did he wonder where his mind went
and when his body would follow?

Rain and pale reminiscences
saturate the grave into mud,
and the boy-now-man points the truck home,
traces of fear in rearview glances
and those who pulse past.
Weathered fingertips brace the wheel,
a soft pat against his thigh,
and a voice whispers: "Just keep it steady."

~~~~~

Pennies

Indian heads and wheat backs
collected like lint
before she slept each afternoon,
scattered across the spread
to entertain the two-year-old
while she dreamed.
He popped one coin
like candy, turned blue,
and learned the lesson well.
For fifteen years and more, she traded
half her weekly salary for
tarnished copper and silver
and allowed him to touch

the prize once a week,
promising to share the riches
some day.

Now she believes she can beat
the creditors with law briefs
and the kid's crisp dollars.
If the worst happens, she says,
Check the walls.
I'm sixty years old.
Why can't we get along?
Copper bites his tongue.

Acquainted

Anyone

Anyone would do.

Anyone at all
with the best music:
we danced, we lay:
Anyone would do.

Anyone at all
to talk:
the VW stuck
on the beach,
that bastard cop, grinning
at Debbie's open blouse:
Anyone would do.

Anyone at all
for truth or dare:
down the street
in my underwear,
found reason to lose them
in dark gulf water:
Anyone would do.

Anyone at all
to sit with me:
numbers fuzz
and surf breaks on
late night shores
of three jiggers, clogged
with stuck VWs,
shirts and pants
on bone-white sand,
giggles between
dunes, beer cans,
condoms, diplomas,
marriages, kids,
divorce, death:
Anyone would do.

Anyone at all.

Johnny

His hands clench into fists,
teeth gnashing until his face glows red,
eyes glaring up from lowered face,
that practiced, possessed mask that's frightened before.
Days ago, his mother raged,
I'm damn sick of coming here
time and again because of you
being in trouble.
Should've never been born.
His face burned red then, too,
but embarrassment filled the eyes,
his gaze locking with mine a moment too long.

He refuses to complete assignments,
drawing, instead, thin feminine figures,
with entrails bursting:
a space mutant,
a robotic hero,
a miniature monster with pointy head,
tiny letters in a word bubble crying,
help.
He drums on his leg and then scribbles
on the page he'll submit in place of his work,
Miss Teacher, I like you.
I dont know WTD.
The bell rings, and he's into the hallway,
rage simmering
for attention
that makes him feel
at home.

~~~~~

And Music for Jeff

Miles splinter the line
as the voice, tired and cracked,
drawls, "Guess it'll be another
six years at some school reunion…"
The cat brushes my leg for

attention in my excitement.
"Any kids?"
"A twelve-year-old dog—
and bare scalp where hair used to be."
"And music?"
"Better than working a goddamn
nine-to-fiver, sucking up
to bastards smelling of BMWs."
The cat curls in my lap,
purrs in stale kitchen odors.
"And music?"
"Still trying, trying. It's like
writing, man. You got to pay some
shit-can load of dues before
they decide to listen to you."
The cat nuzzles my chin,
marking undefined territory.
"And music?"
"Fuck 'em. I do what I do, and I like it.
I average twenty bucks a week, but gigs,
when I get 'em, pay good, real good.
I eat. Usually.
Hey, call me sometime. Read me something."

The phone lies dead in its cradle
as the cat drops to the floor,
content to bathe himself in the
pale screen light of a blinking cursor.

~~~~~

For Angie, Waving

Good enough to toss up a hand
in passing,
but that was as far as her
interest in me went.

But her—
I knew her well,
watching from behind a window
as she picked up the neighbor's kids,

or bathed her face in the summer sun,
or chased her old dog up the street,
a laugh bursting from her lips,
her hair bouncing softly against her shoulders.

I watched her again and again
settle school-kid fights
and caress away the pain of her sons,
shunning neither in favor.
And I heard rumors,
twisted tales whispering
parts of her life had soured,
but her face:

Her grin reveled in vital contentment,
a thousand times filling this window pane
that now reflects strangers' eyes,
passing glimpses.
Still, I keep glancing up, expecting
to find her scooting kids into the back seat,
or laughing after that scrawny dog,
or fondly tossing a wave
one last time
in passing.

~~~~~

The Kid at Dusk

Flecks of orange flash under his feet
against my lights as I shift into reverse
to corner him between two houses,
chain-linked from the next street.

Come here, kid!
I'm surprised he does.
I tingle in twilight
as his face slackens,
his eyes widen with fear
and something unreadable.

...could've hit you...middle of

the road...it's dark,
for chrissakes...no
reflective clothing...

These are words I know I say,
but all I hear is rage
with the threat of parents,
this respect-adults voice
suddenly breaking him to tears.

What'd I do, what?
What, what?

I roll up the window,
glare into the rearview,
the a-c blowing winter
against my scarlet, wet face.
I shift into drive,
move into the rust light
of a streetlamp,
hear defiance fade
in the darkness behind me.

~~~~~

shutterwinks

I

She danced,
hands patty-caking
on the dryer door,
pirouettes across the laundry floor,
a flabby shadow
against fluorescent
corpse gray.
She danced.

II

The music
rose in her mind

like a butterfly,
dipping behind picture windows.
Sweat glistening,
she collapsed into
a puddle of luminescent wax
that suddenly transformed again,
rising, rising,
the butterfly
lifting her by
her fingertips.

III

She bowed once, twice,
snaking cool hands
over gray pimpled flesh,
lips a river of kisses thrown,
hair spinning wildly,
sneakers tossed aside,
jeans a ruffled pile on the floor.
A black hole in the
light of a single bulb,
she sank back into her room,
melting to applause.

IV

Old woman spreads
a hand over her temple,
fingers swollen, nails black,
elbow resting on cracker-thin table,
eyes shading memory;
she sighs, shifting
a crooked jaw.
The hair on her arms
wave in brittle
cotton candy wisps as she
glides to see the dancer,
a pale reflection
against her window,
the Maytag silent,
the plastic hamper empty.

The Waiting Room

He's staring,
deep-set, haggard eyes
peering out from unshaven face.
Finally, I look up, a simple act
to acknowledge the man's existence,
but he takes it as an opening.

"She's scared all right," he says, referring
to someone in one of those sanitized rooms.
"She didn't want to let go of my sleeve."
The others here keep their eyes buried
safely in old magazines.
"We been married ten years now," he says.
"We were both sixty-five then."
Shakes his ragged head. "Both widowed,
but she shoulda divorced her old man early on."

The doctor said an hour in surgery
to make sure all the tissue's out,
the uterus clean, undamaged.
After another hour in recovery,
we can go with his blessings
to try again in a few months.
If at first…

"He used to beat the hell out of her. Used a cane.
I ain't never once touched her in anger."
He sucks his lips.
"Piece of cancer, you know,
but the doc, he said he could just cut it off.
You married?" I nod. "She here?"
I look at my book, but he leans in close.
"Better love her, young feller, and show her."
He settles back, eyes on the door to surgery.
"Ten years ain't much. Hardly nothin'."

Charlie, Passing

A pause?
Sure, Charlie,
a tip of the hat,
a wink of the eye—
I don't mind the wait.
I'll pull onto the shoulder
for you in your victory
as hundreds did for Uncle
in his.

The paper ran words such as
"struggling" and "minor"
and names of one or two
people he left behind—
but they said so little, Charlie.
When those who had been given
an earlier chance finally looked,
they could not praise enough,
could not award enough—
maybe because they knew too well
who drove Uncle to reject them.
I can't say for certain,
but I believe
I sometimes hear Uncle laughing.

Charlie? Yes,
I'll curb my car.
You deserve that much
for making it
as far as you did.
Too bad you
closed your eyes
before you saw
the respect you merit
from strangers like me
along this road
when it counts least.

Cheerleading

The houses on this street are like unexplored planets.
The woman next door told me she can't figure why
she had the kid, "though I don't *regret* it."
Lost a lot of weight in the last year.
Keeps throwing up. Says she wants
to get as thin as the woman across the street,
the former cheerleader who jogs and lifts weights
and works for her papa's business.
Says she's lost enough to wear the cheerleader's clothes:
"Trust me. She can afford to lend me outfits."
I see her at the cheerleader's occasionally,
around dusk when the cheerleader is pruning bushes
or stretching her brown body on a lawn chair,
sipping a wine cooler.
Last time, she borrowed a halter-and-shorts outfit,
went out alone to boogie, she said,
leaving the son with Dad. Says Dad wants
another kid. "I told him no way."
Shakes her head. "But I don't know.
I just need to get my figure right,"
and her hands roll over tiny breasts,
stroke down thin, wrinkled thighs.
She spots the cheerleader and starts over,
but the cheerleader gets into her car,
backs out of the driveway,
wiggling her fingers in a faint wave
as she speeds away alone.

~~~~~

Émeute
—For Andrew

I simply had to come over,
says the woman in rattlesnake boots.
That piece, she clicks, it speaks
to my inner child, and I want you
to know how I feel before I go.
A toothy grin, a press of soft flesh,
and she leaves you in a sea of witnesses

106

who carry invitations like flash cards.
Eyes linger at waists, glance at wrists,
float across bordered images like mist.

Some frightening quality to each,
a woman whispers, and the man with the baby
sighs his personal losses to the matted goat
who appears more like a guest and not a vision.
The college girl hovers at the spiked bowl
while the writer hawks his books to anyone asking,
What kind of work do you do?
And the fat woman dealing antiques
swears by the slimming qualities
of makeup and black blouses:
What would you charge to do a bust of me?

You know each musician, each artist,
each engineer and executive alike,
one way or another. Their voices carry you
toward "sex" and "lust" and "mama," swinging
you around slowly to catch
snatches of smiles as punch spots
the framework of your talent.
The goat's eyes glow in this musty loft air,
and you breathe, *Who are these people?*

~~~~~

Webs

I hear distance in her voice,
a wish unspoken,
a sigh withheld.
A spider ascends
the refrigerator door,
its weightless rise wasted on
a spectator too jaded
to be impressed by miracles.
Her words are drops of warm sweat
seeping through frigid plastic.
The sound would make me cry
if tears were not too thin for pain.

And…and,
she was saying something light,
a laugh tagged onto a word
in a void that has spun
a web of lace around my soul,
softly, gently suffocating.
And…and,
she was saying something sad,
a moan in her throat,
a plea that digs into emotions
smothered in darkness,
disguised as emptiness.

I pinch the spider's strand of silk
and twirl it in a private circus,
lifting it up, up,
wondering if spiders get dizzy.
I set it gently on top of the refrigerator
and collapse into a chair
as it stretches threads to the wall,
linking, binding steel and wood,
like words between people.

~~~~~

His Bed

In that room, that night without sleep,
with the roar of the a-c below the window
and the rumble of rap from some distant house,
I came to understand.

The bed still caressed him even a week after
he'd become ashes tossed into wind,
the pillow bearing the weight of his head,
comforter wrinkled into the rough shape of his body.
Shells and rocks and trinkets on the nightstand,
flowers and stems and decorations beside
the small toolbox on the floor,
a small trunk stuffed with receipts thirty years old,
bearing witness to possessions long discarded—

each rock, each flower, each scrap of paper
told me more about him
than I had learned during his life.

In a central, quiet room,
his partner slept, raptly unaware
of the beat and drone outside the window
where I watched the dark grow deeper.
A picture of the two together lay
half-buried in shredded receipts,
my gaze from the foot of the bed
going to that image repeatedly through the night:
He waded into the ocean's edge
as his partner pointed toward something
caught up in the tide.

Long after dawn, his partner's door opened,
and footsteps padded to the bathroom
but not into this room
where I had begun to pack, unsupervised,
leftovers into boxes
filling with a past now viewed
in a different light.
I packed the picture last,
securely wrapped, and left that room,
a life's impression still clinging to a bed
where I had found no rest.

~~~~~

Jennifer

She roosts on the sofa,
like the crow I saw
on my way home.
It perched in the top
of a barren oak,
head twisting, scanning,
wishing (for all I knew)
it could call that tree *home*.
The wind gusted,
and the limb shivered,

shaking itself free,
sending the crow
circling into gray sky.

It's time for another adventure,
I mutter: *Sorry,* and, gently, I push
her away, push away what someone
taught her, that spontaneous hug,
small mouth open against the fly.
My wife hangs up the phone and says,
I told him we'd have her there at ten.
They can't say no, not after lying to us.

Her eyes redden, she says goodbye
in the parking lot, and I take the girl in.
Jennifer's hand vanishes into the case worker's.
"Is there a daddy at my new home?"
she asks. "I want to give him a hug."
The door behind me opens,
and I shiver against the draft
as she rounds a corner, gliding,
seeking the nest.

~~~~~

All Part of It

He sets his empty plate
beside hers on the coffee table,
pats his belly and sinks into the couch,
apologizing in advance for falling asleep.
We don't mind, content ourselves
to snatch winks as we pretend
to watch *The Wizard of Oz*
between commercials.

The day:
A stroll around a mountain lake
to catch Spring sprouting her gentle head
above the leaves of Winter;
and later, the loan of their truck,
the loan of some muscle,

tired sighs, toasting mugs.

(I once heard a story about friends
who watched each other grow old
one sunny afternoon, how their eyes
refused to dim in the face of mortality.)

He zips down giant, snow-covered dream slopes
as we nibble banana bread
and Dorothy skips to the end of the Rainbow.

She punches him, all laugh,
and we wave so long from the porch,
the light stretching our shadowed hands
out to touch them, to stroke the part
that has made us richer.

~~~~~

Connecting Lots

Rising like cooling ash
from grass and weeds,
fireflies. He says,
The acreage would be just right
with a house up front,
horses in back.
Put a picket fence around it,
get the horses in before it's zoned.

He mows his connecting lot
at dusk with baby
in a backpack.
A slung stick once cut
her forehead. He screamed,
Grow up.

He has his eye on that land
where fireflies ignite,
but his wife's tight, he says,
and they're having problems draining
rain water from under their house.

111

Mainstream

The wind leans against the glass,
and the frame groans.
He's at his desk, eyes half-closed.
The crystalline sky
has brought autumn finally to school.
The a/c is no longer needed,
but the air is stuffy with bodies.
Pencils scratch,
voices hum,
and teachers peck at keyboards.
He's heard the word *mainstream*,
resents all it implies,
though he isn't sure exactly what it means
beyond tests that are never hard
and the chance to sleep whenever he wants.

The glass pulses with the wind.
He hears giggles,
and he realizes he squeaked,
that eyes are on him.
The wind presses,
threatening to burst the glass.

~~~~~

No Good Thing

He persists for two, three years,
then tumbles back in.
Never recalls
the months that follow,
but his wife tells him
about late nights and vomit
and shouting matches
that bring lights on
in neighbors' houses.
His kids sometimes look at him
as though he's a stranger.
The house doesn't feel the same.

The Baptists' roadway wisdom screams
God Will Withhold No Good Thing
To A Man Who Walks Uprightly.
With squalid breath
and hollow eyes, he tries
(God must know *that* by now),
but he's weary of half-veiled
glances caught in the tops
of scuffed black shoes.
He's thirsty and prays the kids and wife
will distract him until the sweat dries
and the night loosens its grip.
He licks salt from his lips
and counts the heartbeats to sunrise.

~~~~~

Moving

The husband wants
one last plant,
but its roots have sliced
through the plastic pot
to grip the earth.
You want to see
my empty house?
I nod toward my feet,
covered in fresh cut grass.
I'd dirty the carpet, I say.
Missy helped us build this place,
hammering nails into the deck,
and her barely ten years old.
Three years straight,
the girl ran up our steps
with candy, Christmas wrap,
and more to sell, grinning,
knowing I'd say no.
Once, a firecracker
popped somewhere nearby,
and she winced,
said she hated guns.
My wife says, *I'd want to stay.*

Where rooms echo her voice,
I ask, where shadows fool,
and every carpet stain's
a teardrop?

Come in, take a look.
I smile, shake his hand,
thankful I have mowing to finish
and rooms not as crowded
as those in that empty house.

~~~~~

When a Neighbor Dies

The couple from across the street
thought it would be a good idea—
whatever the folks
on our block could spare.

Her image is as fresh as yesterday,
her voice still ringing echoes,
hardly the distant memory she was
branded less than a week after.

We dig into our pockets,
fish out a fiver,
sign the card and ask what
will they buy in remembrance.

"We simply want her kids and husband
to have the cash," they say,
as if money can ease our conscience
for not using time when it mattered most.

~~~~~

The Park at One

The boy rips two braces
from the backstop,
freezes:

"Get away from there,"
someone shouts
from an apartment
bordering the field.

The boy is motionless,
eyes searching windows;
voice, silent.

The boy lifts one brace,
wobbles it to the other end of the park,
props it on
a bench and the ground,
and straddles it,
bouncing, bouncing.

The brace finally gives,
splinters,
and the boy wanders away.

~~~~~

Quake

She stands in the doorway,
determination melting,
shoulders racking.
Aftershocks rumbled
even here,
thousands of miles from the
epicenter.
Buildings rocked,
communications jumbled.
We forget
the mortgage,
the electric bill,
the car note—
and wait
for the call that doesn't come.

On Reading *"Émeute"* to the College Girl

She switches on the speaker phone.
Laughter dizzies, and the voice goes.

And goes.

I speak exactly as she expects,
monotone moron with a message.
The speaker's off, and she says
she's getting married in the fall.
The hesitancy I've heard before is still there,
and I wonder if answers can be found
cowering in corners at parties
or submerged in the sweat of dark rooms.

Andrew asks why she makes me so nervous.
I tell him I've never cared for mirrors.

~~~~~

Reconnecting

She's a widow, she tells me,
her husband killed in a chopper crash.
The phone line hisses.
I had a crush on you back then,
when you sat in the front row.
And I had a crush on you, she says,
but she doesn't recall
my card at Valentine's, the way
she snapped those eyes around, angry.
Her words are cautious these decades later,
clipped as she appoints a time for drinks.
I recall her face, that girl of eight,
wonder if time has treated her better
than the trails it's carved in my face.
I dream of possible pasts,
miles clicking off
midlife sins.

Running

He doesn't jog anymore.
He prefers the sanctity of the living room,
the television where vengeance is swift,
the bad guys' hearts cut out,
their heads blown off, the way it should be.

He used to go before dawn, but job and family
and long hours took care of that.
He then took it up after work,
escaping a few minutes on the high
of hard breaths and a fast heart.

A good neighborhood, middle-class,
but car doors flew open at dusk,
and three men encircled,
laughing, knives whipping, slashing,
a bat swinging. He folded himself,
coughed blood, heard tires squeal away,
others roll up, blue light flashing.
His last thought: The cops saw,
stopped them from finishing it.

Two metal pins incapacitate one wrist.
And his attackers? The police botched it,
he says. They're still out.
This morning, he is at the typewriter,
hunt-and-pecking with his good hand,
when he stops and stares down
at the growing pudginess under his shirt.
He rolls the bad wrist, shakes his head,
and hopes something good's on the tube tonight.

~~~~~

Soul

From broken shoots,
new green springs.
It's a sturdy plant,
she says to him, *enviable*.

Mother, she cries in dreams,
give me a soul of bamboo.

Mornings bloom
with the essence
of her mother's fingertips
lingering on her cheek,
damp with the mist of memory.

~~~~~

Stranger, We've Changed the War

I have put away two bottles of wine.
Years ago, I went to war
at home;
my friend, to another world.
I marched in streets,
fighting;
he marched in jungles,
fighting.
Who was the better soldier?

(Stranger,
I am drunk.
Otherwise, I am hopeless.)

I have put away three bottles of wine,
a lifetime.
I'll sleep in a bed of vomit
with rats tonight.
I will dream of marches,
of children,
of old women,
of students,
of soldiers and soldiers.
Tomorrow I will drink a gallon of
wine and pretend
new reasons I did not go,
new reasons my friend did not return.

John

The rows aren't easily defined,
but they are there,
herbs thick and flowering,
vegetables lush and ripening.
He weeds the dying
so the healthy plants
will produce more than he dreamed.
He pauses, back slightly hunched,
and listens: the breeze
sifts through the garden
like a hymn on the lips of children.

He sinks his hand into the earth,
turning, cherishing,
thankful for the harvest.
He cups a tomato in his palm
and hears his mother whisper
from behind the decades.
He blinks eyes gritty with time
and sees her standing with
his father beyond the terrace.
He cradles the tomato to his chest
and settles at the garden's edge,
his nails caked with dirt,
tender leaves kissing
his shoulders with bouquets
of dill and peppermint.

~~~~~

The Mark

Tears gather in a breath of names and places.
With these tears, we have laughed,
touched our pasts too deeply,
and lapsed into silence,
a single, gentle clasp of hands.
The trio behind us chuckles
about things that don't matter,
things that will redden eyes

in twenty years.

I reached for her
back then and never let go,
even when the move split us
for what should have been forever.
I stare, she looks; when our eyes meet,
we glance away, shyly,
elementary kids still playing games.

We're a week apart in age,
two pebbles dropped into this ocean
at nearly the same moment.
Thank you, I say.
She flashes between grin and frown,
hands folded together,
fingers kneading unconsciously,
says she wants to grow up,
to make her mark.
My fingers curl into my palms,
aching to dry the tears she fights,
but how can I explain marks already made?

In the parking lot, we embrace,
whisper *goodbye. Someday*, she promises,
the demons will give up the chase.
Thirty-three years ago,
her glance radiated through my soul
like ripples in a pool,
circles of eternity,
but demons have a way of sliding under the tide.

~~~~~

Slices

I split the apple into quarters,
but she didn't notice the blood on the blade
or the subtle motion of thumb to mouth, cleansing.
Our children giggled, ate the apple,
then raced away for the swings.
She and I spoke of things we'll never understand,

of gods and demons and women and men,
of love and understanding,
of responsibility and longing.

It is that bitter taste of blood I recall now,
so strangely wonderful as I aimed my camera
to capture the soft, gracious way she rose
to convince her daughter
to smile for my lens,
burning image into memory.

~~~~~

Slices, Too

It's the bitter taste of blood I still recall,
even now, three years after
our daughters vied for those succulent slices
on the table between us.
The apple's sugar stung
the flesh my knife flayed open,
and a drop of blood smeared
my camera's release as the lens captured
those beautiful girls in time.
You're there, too,
in the spark in your daughters' eyes,
and I understand how blood,
in all its sweet bitterness,
runs thick.

~~~~~

Surface Tension

Orange glittered hair,
pierced brow and navel, snide grin,
mischievous, challenging eyes,
needle words, pushing, pushing,
yet his notebook bears
Mother Teresa and the caption,
the smile is the beginning
of love.

Rosé tinted glasses

Another Drunk

—For Mr. Carver

Drunks have been done to death.
Raymond took care of that,
so don't expect me to add much here.
Still, my old man could
put away some booze,
but God and I know he was no drunk.
Just liked the buzz
from time to time;
still does as far as I know.
Mom, she'd swear he was
the sloppiest drunk
to put lips to a bottle,
though she never had to worry
after the divorce;
just liked to because the role
of victim came easily.

I like to drink
from time to time.
A good way to zap a feeling,
if you see my meaning,
and God and I know it makes
the day go down easier.
I could, in fact,
use a tall one right now,
but I don't have time.
That's why I envy the drunks.
That's why I envy Raymond,
even though he learned how to live.

~~~~~

Waiting for the Post

I

I can't believe you've stood
there
all morning.

You could've been
cleaning
up after yourself,
doing something
useful.
Can the mail be that
damned important?

II

Ghosts dance on the window
pane,
spread and fly
as the sun splits
condensation into
single atoms.

III

Winter
comes in
whispers
that chill
grave-sitters like me—
I ache for warmth:
this comforter only
insulates
the icy
gnawing
at my bones.

IV

You've been waiting
long enough,
don't you think?
Take the rag;
dry the window.

V

I drew faces

on frosty panes
when I was a kid.
Granny would warn me
not to dirty the windows,
then laugh at my finger-sketched faces:
withered,
mummified.

VI

You're still
there?
(I have drunk a half-bottle
of wine,
watching droplets
evaporate.)
God, you look like
a ghost.

VII

Granny knew nothing about
atoms.
She would stare
through windows
for hours,
talking to her husband,
dead for 38 years.
Once,
she touched a pane:
the ghost gathered itself into
a single droplet
at her fingertip.

VIII

Draw the drapes.
(I drink,
sift through bills,
gravesite offers, expiring
subscriptions.)
Draw the drapes, I say.

It's as cold as death
in here.

IX

The panes tempt
twilight moisture from the room,
gathering drops for
tomorrow.
I nestle the bottle between my lips,
sink deeper,
deeper,
always deeper
into the comforter,
shudder,
wait and hope the ghosts
will dance again.

~~~~~

Spare Change

"Spare some change for something to eat?
A piece of chicken? A slice of bread?"
He draws on the cigarette,
eyes drilling the beg
with desire and loathing.

I turn away, and he coughs,
"How 'bout a dollar, just a dollar?"
For what? More smokes, a bottle of wine?
I hear him exhale a cloud
as my knuckles around the bus stop post
grow as yellow as the nicotine
that stains his fingernails.

He curls his back against the bank,
slides down, forearms propping on his knees,
his eyes meeting every passing stranger.
In my half-hour for the bus,
he asks a dozen people,
"Change? For something to eat?"

and coins fall into his hand,
disappear into his jacket.

He lights another Marlboro
as the bus screams around the corner.
"Hey man, just your pennies.
I'm hungry."
The doors hiss open. I climb the stairs,
dig into my pocket, come up with fare.
I slip into a seat, glance out
through the glass that separates us.
He winks at me and rasps,
"God bless you."

A piece of chicken;
a slice of bread.

Twenty minutes later,
I am in the supermarket
where my credit's good
and the cashiers never look me in the eye.

~~~~~

Under the Banyan

Under the banyan,
gnarled and leafless,
in black coolie,
straw hat dangling down her back,
string taut around her neck,
she huddles,
a negligence of bone and skin,
eyes narrowed,
thin, black umbrella spread.
She waits.

The jogger circles
the park,
knees grinding,
heart hammering.

Coughs rack her shoulders
as he passes
again,
again.
She draws up her legs,
feet flat before her,
grass edging up
brittle ankles.
She waits.

Around,
around,
he feels her eyes
slice through
his heaving lungs.
Sweat bathing his chest,
agony ripping his knees,
he collapses

under the banyan.
Shrinking in the
shadow of her umbrella,
he waits.

~~~~~

Beach

Don't get sand on the carpet,
shake it off,
wash before you enter.
Surf breaks fifty yards away
and gulls glide over
eroded dunes,
sea oats,
and miles of sand
as fine as sugar.
They've trucked in sod,
squares of grass
as lush as a putter's dream
moving here, craving the beach,
but too attached to the mower.

My cat,

the eunuch,
purrs under my scratching fingertips,
a reminder of how short a distance
I have come
in such a long span:
I have only
memories
now to rape my daydreams.

And of course,
my cat, purring,
scratching,
sleeping
while I sip coolers—
drowning images
that sink
to the bottom of the glass.

~~~~~

Closets

In the Taco Bell, the woman
with glasses, wrinkled eyes, and tired smile
says she'll be on radio
this National Coming Out Day of celebration,
though that ring on her finger tells me
her topic won't be fags.
Before I came in here for burritos,
I heard two lesbians on the public
station's talk show, fielding
callers' divine knowledge:
Depression, drug abuse, reasons, excuses.

The woman at the table across from me,
the one whose makeup crinkles around the nose
with every crunch of taco—
I wonder what home life is like,
the skeletons she must hide.
Has she performed for hubby dear

while preferring sleep to the rub?
And what about his buddy? Has she an eye?
Or maybe she's considered her lady friend—
no, no, there's that ancient ring
and the indignant glare at the long-haired boy
prancing toward the counter.

"Must go," the woman says, and she leans
to kiss her female companion on the cheek.
I saw that, lady.

~~~~~

A Dime's Worth

(with apologies to Mr. Harburg)*

And so we worry
about the blue-collar,
the wage-earner,
the poor,
wading through our leaves of grass,
along our Walden shores.
In or out of the grave,
we bear the blame when they suffer—
we who believe in the good of humanity.

As I repay the loan
that financed the paper
on the wall behind me, pay
the electric company,
the city,
the state,
the federal tax machine,
the mechanic,
the grocery clerk,
Red Cross,
Goodwill,
United Way,
the beggar on the street,
the guy cutting across three lanes
who draws a .45 for *his* mistake,
I know in my soul,

I deserve the blame for
the burdens,
the sorrows,
the anger.

I wallow with my brothers and sisters,
assured that we must understand.
But when I crawl away from a fight
to hide within my degreed humanity,
why do I feel less a person than
the ones laughing at me,
the ones I am told to pity?

*E.Y. Harburg wrote the lyrics for "Brother, Can You Spare a Dime."

~~~~~

At this Distance

At this distance,
we look the same, I'm certain:
side to face,
two bodies in a lock of air,
spinning dust
between dirty cars.

At this distance,
we are
jerks fighting.
We are not
the redneck
and professor,
one who made a mistake,
one who pointed it out
and paid as target.

At this distance,
we're just something
to call the cops about,
or (more likely)
to avoid,
to ignore.

Enemies

My skin is yellow, she says,
pressing her forearm against mine.
She is testing, I think,
drawing attention to differences—
the roundness of my eyes,
the smallness of her breasts,
the reach of our fingers.
She plays the movie,
fire raining down from Allied planes,
children dying slowly, so slowly,
drawing tears from her eyes—
and mine.
She touches my cheek,
draws her fingertip to her lips,
whispers, *We taste the same.*

~~~~~

When Hawaiian Girls are Grinning

They gawk at the end of the world,
on the edge of existence, the lie's
thin blade poised to slash.
They savor soft *mauka* rains, gentle trades
as dark hands and swaying hips weave
hokus-pokus dreams in the safe district.

They yearn to live with a rainbow
springing from their doorstep.
(Hundred'll get you a night with the grass skirt.)
They numb themselves with dreams of
native smiles, their dollars
blindly nurturing the veiled myth:
this land, this people, this paradise.

Holidays

Baptists slam the door
in their faces, they say,
but I sense respect
for having chosen honesty.
They are Witnesses witnessing
to a man who's long stopped
hoping, who dissects reality
until stigmata bleed tears.
Most people don't know the truth
about Christmas, one of the women says,
and I say you can herd sheep into fire.
She twists her hair over one breast,
sweat beading on her forehead and neck,
sparkles sliding into her dress.
She licks her lips, nods at the brick house.
The Church of Christ man damned us,
she says, but my porch is fair game
to Witnesses and to preachers
with soft palms, big hair,
and evangelical grins.
The one in the flowered print dress
rolls her eyes skyward. You believe?
I shrug. A beetle scurries onto the walk
and dies under her foot. I say,
We all make sacrifices.

~~~~~

Hurricane

Nail the boards sturdy
over windows
for gales will rip
at their hold
to shatter panes,
to wreck the shell.
Strike the best defense,
the hardest core.
And wait. Wait
undeceived by the

silent eye that
beckons you out.
Wait until it has
passed you by, hungry
for those too naïve
to raise their guard.

~~~~~

As I Imagined

I returned last night,
floating on time melting:
golden fingers—long, sensual—
stroking feathery hair
tousled by her laughter.

She blushed as her eyes
clouded with high school.
She called out a name,
and her son appeared,
smacking peanut butter and jelly,
nodding in time to metal.
He cocked his head, said hi,
then evaporated into his music.

I held her weathered hand
and ached to stroke
her wrinkled mouth, her furrowed eyes.
When she asked,
I declined to meet the man.
Then she smiled, and I saw
the face of a girl flicker,
felt the heartbeat of a boy fade.

~~~~~

The Immigrant

The combination takes ten minutes,
he says, and he offers to cook
a pizza for the man.

The gun waves in quivering hands.
The cash register—open it, open it!
The drawer slides, a door swings,
the hand tightens, the hammer falls,
and the immigrant feels his teeth shatter,
steel fragments lodge in his jaw.

Dentures cover well enough,
and he's still got a taste for pizza,
but the public's a different story.
Chewing, he can feel
metal grate against bone
as suspicion scans all eyes
that set a path across his.
Seems he recalls expecting
something different with freedom.

~~~~~

Immortality

She whispers to the woman beside her,
This house smells like Kyoto temples,
but the house is centuries younger
than ancient floors her feet have walked.
He stands in the doorway,
pretends he's touched such aged wood,
those halls shaped by divine prayers
of Buddhist monks.
The stiff breeze invades,
rustling his hair,
sweeping back her perfume
and the sweat of hardened wood.
He lifts his face,
his eyes tearing against the sky,
beyond vast clouds that scatter
on the breath of space,
where moments are forever
and dreams await for the taking.

Kimono

They skirt along histories,
coo against the bindings.
Her gaze flashes around the room
as young hands grasp her silken skirts—
traditional dress in this country where
tradition serves as quaint distraction.
Curious fingers stroke
down blossoms of cherry,
the softness of fabric,
the aroma of flesh.
She whispers to the children,
It's so tight, this wrap.

~~~~~

Light

Light streams
a blinding beam against Spring
(March is the cruelest month of all,
wallowing in what has perished
a million times,
resurrecting ghosts of ghosts.),
a casual reminder, a razor against
fragile skin,
a voice trapped inside tears
from pain, pain, pain
mere steel cannot lay bare.
Crimson stabs through the sky,
showers pull flowers into
memories budding for slaughter.

Light streams
a blinding beam against Autumn
(September is the cruelest month of all,
mocking what has wallowed
as ghosts in the form of beauty.),
a razor sliding against the jugular,
pulsing with whim,
a voice trapped outside crying

for escape, escape, escape
that flows as a crimson shower,
streaming—a desert flood
glistening against the skin like tears
that feed the shriveled blooms of March.

~~~~~

The medic

lifts a piece
of bone and meat,
peers into
the skull,
and, sighing a grin,
mumbles, *an inch*
higher and the
soldier might've
hit the enemy.

~~~~~

Metallic Wisdom

Our progress is undeniable:
you won't find peace
nailed to a cross
in our world.

We've bought ourselves
three extra decades each,
the wonder of science.
We've cured a million diseases;
we'll cure a million more.

We've spawned the ages of wisdom:
Plato, Socrates, Confucius, Jesus, Buddha, Gibran,
and the rest,
even our few modern versions
(which we may snicker at now,
but we mean no harm,
no harm).

With our wisdom in hand, we have
compressed miracles into aerosol cans,
brushed our lips with the petals of a rose's atom,
massaged our minds at the edge of the universe...

But none of that matters.

We are the man in the median
with a bullet through his brain,
the man who put it there
when the light was red.

~~~~~

Mistakes

The fireflies are shy tonight—
a rare flicker here,
another there:
summer has heat enough
without their furnaces.

They will soon abide in
darkness until spring,
when they will again
speckle the air
on moon-scarce nights,
when one will
crawl
into my house
and make my heart
spin
as I
grind
it under heel,
mistaking it for
a roach.

Music

For some reason, it happens.
And it happens.
The mood comes from nowhere—
a fragrance,
a discordant bird,
a certain combination of notes
from the turntable,
the way the breeze moves,
or doesn't—
and you're back to that night,
your mother's screams,
your father's curses,
your hands covering your ears, shielding,
until—goddamn it, goddamn it—
a hand strikes the face
of someone you love, and you're there,
right there,
right where you should not be,
cementing the odor,
the shrill little syllables,
that bird outside,
that record on the stereo,
that heavy riff and high vocal,
that combination of notes, of notes—
goddamn it!
Won't someone
turn down the noise?

~~~~~

New Orleans TV, 2005

Images meld
one into another,
but the sound is muted.
A woman wades through waist-high water
that was once her street.
Politician raises a bass and grins for the cameras.
Suits and immaculate faces,
ears plugged with constant instruction,

video heads asserting, asserting.
Images, disconnected, connected,
irrelevant in the dark of light,
where no one knows
who's watching what.

~~~~~

For the New Order

They give me a double take,
confounded.
Is my skin a sin?
Guilt by association?
I've raised no flags,
caged no person,
denied even fewer.
But let us forget that I,
my brothers and sisters,
am present tense.
Assume that I am past.
Charge me with
ancestral transgressions,
pervert "I have a dream"
into a nightmare of slurs,
of threats of "overcoming,"
disguising bigotry as reform.

In the meantime,
pass me the can, please.
I must dispose of these eyes
that once reflected no color.

~~~~~

Under a North Wind

A north wind
slid over the kids in the field—
their sticks,
their march,
their chant.

The window
behind his desk shimmered.
He winked, milky film sliding back,
and she shivered, unprotected
from the frigid draft
through the cracks.

The chant rippled
against the glass.
The man apologized to her,
said circumstances were beyond
his control. It isn't my fault.

A north wind
prickled her skin,
the chant rising, falling,
growing, calling,
chill howl battering
the glass cages that conceal
blind managers who cower
behind plays of time.

And she tittered,
defying the sharpened sticks,
ramming forward,
brave enough to call the bluff.

~~~~~

Old Cat

crouches,
claws drawn beneath
a fold of newspaper
unworthy of fish;

old cat

peeks out
from under tattered edges—
like a wino

caught between
Bottle and Mission,
worshipping the shield
with no one to share
his joy.

~~~~~

Leon, Passing
(originally entitled "Old Friend")

Cuddled in that tattered shirt
to ward off the cold
pressing just beyond the wall,
he has begun to smell.
He fidgets and licks the sore
as sleep fails to come.
He nearly died twelve years ago
when his plumbing clogged.
Tubes, tablets, and tenderness
worked him through,
but he's an old man now.
His hips are gone.
His eyes are dull.
His curiosity has slipped away.
He smells.

He stirs as my fingers meet his brow,
then lift him from the box.
Relax, old friend.
Forget the cold beyond,
that festering spot in your side.
Feel the strokes upon your back,
the warm caress
as the needle slips you
into the place where I
will someday follow.
Sleep.
Sleep.

Fritz

Back there, a rich patch
of green grows where
I once played basketball.
Hello, old friend, I whisper.
Dad played last,
shooting hoops and
asking why I had stopped.
He pounded the fresh,
turned soil underfoot, packing
it solid around the carcass.
Twenty-nine years, I've
refused to step up to the line,
to make that last free-throw.
Hello, old friend,
I mutter again, and sink
my fingers into the
lush, green patch.
The grass is as thick as fur.

~~~~~

One of a Kind

Like no other—
No.
What new
can be said
of anything,
of everything,
of nothing?
Singularity, similarity,
illusions of the blind.
Spare incantations.

Just be.
For god's sake,
let be.

Against the Palm

The hummingbird hovered for hours
against the garage ceiling,
unwilling or unable
to find the open door,
finally slipping
through a hole into the attic
to bat itself against a vent.
Its wings moved in slow motion
as I cupped gloved hands around.
It settled, breast against palm,
needle beak slipping
between forefinger and thumb.

Outside, the bird thrummed up
to hover before me for a heartbeat,
as though I were a flower,
then skimmed skyward,
a smudge against blue,
blurring into the forest.

I no longer believe in dreams,
but I wonder if birds
see more than withered faces
and darkened eyes they spark
with miracles.

~~~~~

Parting

I haul the question down
to words muttered
in black alleys that smell of urine,
where the twelve-year-old
kicked out Charlie's teeth
as he coddled rotgut
with leathery fingers.
A window two floors up
slammed shut on laughter
from a TV screen of comics,

joking for the homeless,
and Charlie swigged
and coughed out a chuckle
through blood and drool
as the kid fled into the amber light of
street pimps and honey-babes.

I shiver in the chill of darkness,
mutter that a boy his age
should have been home with his mum and dad,
then bury myself deeper in fur,
pleased that I've done my five-dollar bit
for the wino I find at my door
each Christmas with fingers spread.

In the street, he approaches,
no bottle, a toothless grin
on his stubbled face,
eyes milky with blunted memories,
a backslapping palm raised,
a goodhearted how-are-you rasping.
I'm aware of his other hand
burying itself
in a ratty coat pocket,
finger wrapping around steel,
a barrel rising.
I am spinning, spinning,
convinced that I made a difference.

~~~~~

Pensacola Beach

Fences block off the sand
along the evacuation route
with signs posted:
 "Preservation project, stay off.
Stay off." Small efforts
against footsteps across dunes
missed by the bulldozers
and the builders
and the condos

and the cars with northern tags
and the tourists pink and pudgy.
In summer, locals pay homage
to the concrete and fences
with hopes that this season
will bring the big southern blow
to clean it all away.

~~~~~

Playground boy

gallops toward the merry-go-round,
belt whistling overhead,
free hand yanking up baggy pants,
again, again.
A modern cowboy
or fighter pilot,
perhaps the president,
ready to loose an Armageddon
of armies, navies, and air forces
to kill what needs to be killed
in the name of
freedom and democracy,
vaguely aware,
as the whistle blows,
his pants may fall
to his ankles.

~~~~~

Possum Eyes

It stands erect in headlights,
as if peering directly at me.
Rubber squeals, and I wrestle the wheel,
but there's no place to go:
Stuck in the middle,
an eighteen-wheeler to my left,
a soft shoulder to my right.

I flung myself out of bed last night,

ripped from sleep,
still feeling the thuds,
again, again, again,
the body underneath, working bumper to bumper.
It had stood on its hind legs, eyes gleaming:
It's show time!

Outside, the sun scorches
the barren wind of summer.
The kid next door kicks
his dog in the mouth.
I hear its familiar clipped yelp
as it tries to eat.
I bury my head in the pillow,
searching the darkness
until I find the possum's eyes,
the snarl on its lips, that grin,
that smirk at bravery behind the wheel.

~~~~~

Ready?

It would be ludicrous,
the teacher said,
to run a marathon
without training.
Same with trumpet,
or driving,
or any damn thing worth doing.
In the next room,
a newborn cries,
out of the blocks,
not a clue.

~~~~~

Relics

The sign "Civil War Relics" pulls him in,
eager as though he might spot blood
still clinging to one of the blades.

What is the fascination with things that kill so efficiently?
My father collects guns—pistols, rifles, shotguns,
single-actions, repeaters, you name it—
relishing the ways he could bring a man down.
He opens the unlocked cabinet to show guests,
says he wouldn't hesitate to use one—
no sir, wouldn't hesitate at all.
And this man, headed up that steep stairwell
to the relic room, to view those implements
of our eagerness to take life…
I sense his fascination, feel it pulling,
tempting me with the ability to kill
or be killed.
Just one breath, one twitch of a finger.
I wonder—a hat pin, a frying pan,
a well-placed lug wrench—
why are they missing from the relic rooms?

~~~~~

Someone Said Words are Useless

Floating in from the edge,
a buoy to suspend me above the waves:

I awaken, gasping,
my lungs filled with
the briny water of nightmares,
drawing me into
blackest, drowning depths.

Words are whispered inadequacies,
and, yet, with a single syllable,
I am rising,
shivering into warmth:
I can breathe.

Scrap from an Old Notebook

This is what I found:

These are the empty times,
reaching ever deeper
for gifts and giving,
knowing that each act
is as worthless as a word
hissed on desert wind,
borne without sound
to no one.

That's it. Nothing more.
Nothing.

It's hot today.
Are you listening?
I said, it's hot.

~~~~~

Self-Portrait

I am no Rockwell leaning
leftward to peer
into my own reflection
and paint the image of what
I believe others see me as.
These are days of self-
portraits, I'm told, days
of preparation, but the brush
shakes in my hand as I slip
through the pastels of my wife's care.

My preschool daughter has examined
dried worms in the driveway,
has witnessed a man murder a man
on the TV news.
She cocks a finger at me:
"I killed you, Dad.
I killed you, Dad!"

But she has it wrong:
I am resurrected
by midnight whispers
and watercolors of innocence.

~~~~~

September

September, and already the leaves
have begun to litter the lawn.
In defiance, a single dandelion fires
its golden head above the grass.

The poster on the wall arcs light
across the living room as the sun
sinks west, reflecting golden petals.
Blackbirds screech laments
as they set their wings
to the wind for the long haul.
And there's mischief next door,
the brood plotting tricks for treats,

and, still, neither birdsong
nor the brood's wrongs
shadow this single dandelion,
its golden hue vibrating pulchritude
in defiance of the hum rising
beyond the primordial horizon,
distant, but drawing ever nearer.

~~~~~

Shakes

Faded and scarred by seasons,
this old house needs new shingles—
a dye job, he chuckles,
hand raking through his own gray.

Chipped corners mark the day when she screamed
at the sudden clap of thunder, the rush of wind

lifting a single shingle up and away;
the day the baseball hit hard;
the day he slid to the roof's edge,
the antenna wire in his hand
snapping taut at the last moment.

This old house needs a new roof,
yet he waits, reluctant
to bury the years under new shingles,
drawing out the days
one shake at a time.

~~~~~

Simplicity

Butterfly perches on a white sleeve,
here in this infant grove.
Someday, flutes will be fashioned
from these canes,
but, for now, grass thickens
and new shoots break ground
from spreading rhizomes.

Wind stirs,
leaves susurrate,
butterfly remains.
In this moment,
perfection,
like a single note
charmed from the
emptiness of a notched culm.

~~~~~

Parked
(originally entitled "Space")

Each day,
heads bob, twist, nod,
eyes searching, closing, leaking—
fast-food cartons on dashboards,

tiny plastic bags on bucket seats,
this time
doors locked, windows down;
next time
windows up, doors open—
one soul, sometimes two,
caged between minutes and
white lines sketched on asphalt,
craving privacy
in a world of voyeurs,
circling in search
of a place to park.

~~~~~

Deep Space

I stared into
deep space once,
and understood—
yes. For a moment.

I couldn't focus the scope:
no planet,
no star,
no universe.

I stood in the middle of a grassy
field ravaged by cows.
Miles away, dogs sniffed my scent
and howled.

For an instant,
I could not smell,
could not hear,
could not see
anything.

I was alone
as I am now,
as I will always be.
Yet, not since pointing that scope

toward the speckled fuzz of space
have I seen
as clearly as
the moment when
I saw nothing at all.

~~~~~

Squoze

Between the elevator and escalator,
she was squeezed a bit too tight.
As we paused between
the gems, between
the how-about-something-to-
go-with-that-bottle-of-yuk, between
all the in-between-
got-to-sell-you-anything,
she sighed,
and left,
penny pocketed.

~~~~~

Survival

The rush is on,
four lanes packed
with belching, overheated engines
and accusing glares.
The light's red,
a-c's roaring,
eyes drifting,
and there,
above this glutted intersection,
three sparrows attack a hawk,
diving, climbing, diving again,
the sparrows fitful, desperate.
The limp body in the hawk's beak
is surely dead.
A horn sounds,

the sparrows break away,
the hawk glides into blue to fill his belly,
and cars and trucks move beyond the light,
their drivers headed home
to plates of warm chicken.

~~~~~

The Bird

Fake dew from a water pistol shimmers on yellow petals
as I turn to the van in the street.
The driver calls to me, "Something's wrong with it.
I don't think it can fly." Then I see the bird sitting
directly on the lane marker, as if daring to be hit.
The driver shrugs at my lack of reply,
rolls up her window and drives on.
I leave the camera on the front steps and go
into the street, nudge the bird gently.
It reacts with a hop, barely opening an eye.
I have never seen a bird's eyelids before.
I direct cars around, drivers glaring
from behind cool glass.
A horn sounds, and I'm nudging again,
sending the bird into a fitful battering of wings.
It settles in my yard near the sparkling daffodils.
Knowing nothing to do, I go
inside, telling myself it's only resting.
As I maintain a passing watch from my window,
a boy crosses the street, eyes wide,
a smile glinting. With a stick, he prods
the bird twice before I can open the door.
The boy's gaze is defiant, but he backs away
when I use the word "sick."
At dusk, the bird lifts itself twenty yards,
faltering like a drunkard,
lands in a flurry in the next yard.
I lower the drapes, sink into the couch,
close my eyes.
The following day, my neighbor
is leveling a patch of dirt
as her toddling daughter holds vigil:

the necessary rites.
What good have I accomplished?
Is death easier with an eye dimming on the nest,
or by the rush of a tire or jab of a blunted spear?
She gives the dirt one last whack, packing it down.

~~~~~

The Test

Ms. Taguchi
and Mr. Yates
are working late
when sirens wail.
She cocks her head,
notes the clock.
"Never on time."
From the window,
people: fleas, specks,
dots on a map.
"The trick," she says,
tapping purple
nail to temple,
"is to ignore;
it's so simple."
Mr. Yates shrugs,
slouches to his
swivel chair,
his metal desk,
his overtime.
Ms. Taguchi
straightens,
flashes a smile.

~~~~~

Holiday Traffic

Three shreds of tinsel
glitter from the mirror,
holiday reds winking.
The cameraman fades on the lights,

canned for the six o'clock;
the photojournalist aims,
shutter clicks,
a flash in wet eyes,
page one credit.
Sirens rise, wane, flat-line.

This old truck chugs on,
the woman's face, twisted and streaked,
filling my mirror,
her arms crossed weakly over her chest
as the police motion impatiently,
trying to clear the backlog.

I switch off my radio,
the worn verses of open fires
and roasting chestnuts.
My wife is also clogged in this traffic
on some darkening main artery.
I lean into the driving,
as if will alone
can place her home before
possibility sketches my face
in another mirror,
a different intersection.

~~~~~

Transplant

Far more developed
than I'd expected,
they'd formed
an underground network
that took hours to pull.
Even now,
shoots pop up
here and there,
random reminders of
how we transplanted
the original cuttings,
never suspecting

roots
would never
completely
give way.

~~~~~

Turtle Lawn

"I picked this land up
for less than it cost
to build the lake."
He cocks an ear to
the ripple of a turtle's
head breaking the mirror-slick
surface, leans against the
railing and curses,
having forgotten the pistol.

"Clean out the turtles,
get rid of the snakes,
stock it with catfish,
bass and bluegill;
landscape, cut in roads…"
A woodpecker's hollow rap
skips across the lake
from the timber depths beyond.

"Six lots this side,
five over there.
People pay pretty
for peace and quiet."
The turtle dives,
the pecking silences,
and I hear
babies cry,
mowers whiz,
boat rigs churn.

The Vapor King

Who is this man among so many
sardined into the bus depot?
How can he sit with such dignity
as we maneuver away one by one?
Threadbare cuffs and seams
can't diminish his air of confidence,
his head, crowned with unruly gray,
eyes, staring in certain majesty
as his royal trumpet blares
disdain for social graces.
That is the key, the sticking point,
the thorn that irritates to our undoing:
our innate contempt for such sovereign drafts.

~~~~~

Worth

For what it's worth:

I had a dog as stupid as water,
bounced up on my legs,
ripped my clothes for a pat:
sent that dog reeling,
a chop against the ear for what
it cost me in pants.

For what it's worth:

I had a cat as stupid as dirt,
clawed right through the screen
just to scratch and shit in sand:
sent that cat flying
twenty yards for what
it cost in wire.

For what it's worth,
I tried.
I tried.

Neighborhood Watch

Show time on the block.

The woman next door is acting cocky,
according to the neighbor across the street.
Brags about her husband's completed treatment,
how in six weeks he cured himself of dependence
on prescription drugs and alcohol.
And their friend four houses down the block—
the one whose boy stole the rubber snake
off our blueberry bushes, then joined
Mr. Reform's kids in baptizing
the bushes with gasoline—
he's doing a lot better too,
since his name made the newspaper.
None of them liked the idea—
arrested, possession and selling—
but at least it was buried in D section.
And the people who matter,
they don't read the paper anyway.
What about damage control?
Church and baseball games will suffice.

Monday's trash day.
As I set the recycling container on the curb,
I count fifteen beer cans in Mr. Reform's bin.
Must've had guests. Yes, that's right:
Mr. Controlled Substances was up
for a neighborly visit Saturday afternoon.
Social work, I'm sure:
Mutual reassurance
on the short road to recovery and reform.
A few beers between buddies,
some talk of old times.
And new?

Yard Sale

The girl twists a strand of beads
around a finger and giggles, *I want it.*
A shard of dimming light plays
off musical mobiles and squeaking beds,
an experiment with beads and love.

Will you take a dollar for the Christ?
The coat and slacks he wore the night
he threw the Son at his wife
and chipped a thorn against the bedpost
bring more than the five expected.

This ring—is that a real diamond?
He blinks, wonders about friends
and enemies, and says,
Scrounge the boxes.
Deals galore. Make an offer.
What will you take for the lot?

Time spins. It's only junk.

~~~~~

Flight

Words, phrases scratched on ruled lines,
change places, eliminate themselves,
scream what's right at the moment.

And they fly

For the judgment of cadence,
the accepted standards, the new ways
for old thoughts, the voice in vogue.

And they fly

For the slashing, rehashing,
thrashing, trashing.
Forgotten.

Desire

The results show normal
for all checked, but we know
they couldn't test for everything—
not enough money, not enough time,
not enough probability.
And positives would require decisions.

The hospital's said to be the best,
at least in this area,
and when you've got little else
to choose from, you take the ward tour
with the appropriate ooos and ahhhs,
knowing, but certainly not admitting,
that cash could get you better.

The classes are straightforward,
no promises, only probabilities
quoted by a woman who's worked
both sides of the table.

(And mothers seldom understand
when the loss is yours and not exactly theirs.
They crave first words,
to act as relay,
their own tears more important, somehow,
never mind the years, the planning,
the crib, the paintings on the wall.)

This rented movie is nothing,
a shoot-'em-up, can't-trust-anyone flick.
Her stomach's lopsided,
part of us shifting again,
and tears flood her eyes.
"I just want it to be okay."
I can offer no guarantees—
just a shoulder
and a head full of probabilities,
half-steps short of reality.

Lump

At this point, *It*
is a squirming knot of meat
riding up on her right side,
like a baseball or fist or tiny heel.
And a friend asks,
"Why, in today's world?"

"To give" comes to mind,
but, rather than an answer,
the words sound
more like justification.
What will *It* determine
between womb and stone?
That life is a dance,
psychotic and malleable?
Or an endurance test,
rewards too few?

She lies back on the couch and moans softly,
says *Lump*'s shifting attention.
I cup my hand against her abdomen,
and she nuzzles my chest.
I close my eyes, imagine a face,
wrinkled, red, gooey with wonder,
and she sighs the most basic of whys.

~~~~~

Taxed

State refund came today,
a two-hundred-buck kickback
on our new daughter.
And a statement,
an accounting
for the record,
for next year's tally.

My daughter is growling in her swing,
the carnal sound of my thoughts,

but she's furious over something
that won't matter two minutes from now.
Me? It'll take a lifetime and some.
Like her mother's grandfather,
he died pissed at life.
A year later, the widow
still had to account for him.

We filed our daughter
with the government,
got her a number,
and she's not even four months old.
Maybe that's my problem tonight,
that damn number at the end.

Dementia

Of Mortal Creation

At midnight
I am near the end.
The bottle is dry
except for the spoonful
of spittle that has
drooled from my lips.
I tip my head in praise,
oh god,
and snore.

I am anathema,
for this god's nectar
has performed design's opposite,
has enabled me to
see the world for what
she has become:

stranded, a rock,
her serpents and dogs,
spitting, howling, ripping
all who stroll her
barren shores.

Raped,
drained,
poisoned,
she's turned on us.

Take this bottle,
god of vine,
god of insight,
and fill it with contempt
to fuel this fire
under me.
Bait the howls,
tempt the fangs
and fill my veins
with enough courage
to dance with the Maenads,
to ravage,

to finish this Scylla
of mortal creation.

~~~~~

Atalanta's Legacy

Daughters,
I had you beaten.

Naked,
she lay her naïveté open to me.
"Miraculous,"
they chirped;
they screamed,
"She has met her equal."
But was I
more or less?

I gave only the required.
I could not have been the fool
who fought for "honor"
at the hunt.
Love has never made me
stupid enough to die.

Golden apples as my weapon
(you sneer, call me Cheat),
I won. I won
and made her less
than my equal.

Didn't I?

Lion and Lioness,
our den was never bare.
In our sins,
she served me well,
but her mind was on the future.

Daughters,
I won the race,

but sweet Atalanta
never stopped running;
she has sparked your souls,
fixed your eyes on the line.
Sons hear your footsteps gaining,
feel your breath upon their necks.

~~~~~

Burial Ground

He tells the story
of ghostly whoops
surrounding Uncle
four decades back,
how those cries
drove like a spike
into the ground.
He prods a dirt mound,
unearths trinkets of the dead,
and says he can almost
hear the cries Uncle swore to.
He fondles a piece of clay pot,
says he wants to be buried
with nothing but skin and bones.
 He's afraid the ones who dig
 him up a century from now
will steal his pocket change.

~~~~~

In Shadows, They Cry

Vague apparitions,
she explains,
assemble near the soon-to-die,
faces and features distorted,
darkness shaping, reshaping
all but the eyes which
remain constant,
pleading, accusing,
until she flees

in prayers for strength
to blind herself.
Trembling with knowledge,
she says nothing to those
around whom the darkness gathers,
nor to the darkness itself.
If the shadows clot around me,
I beg her, *please tell me.*
She cries softly
across the ocean that separates us.

Longing in this room,
I whisper to the silence,
さびしい です、 *
and reach for invisible hands.

        *sabishii desu: "I am lonely."

                ~~~~~

Armageddon Sky

A scarlet moon peeks
above the horizon
and lingers long
enough to tempt,
then slides behind
a thin veil of clouds
before the shutter can click.

The photographer, insane
with the knowledge of omens,
searches the sky for the warning,
listens: A dog howls to the bleat
of a siren or to its own curious
realization of time
as the bloody moon rises
behind a world's blinding haze
and the Uzi blasts of a news screen.

The Minotaur's Last Meal

The Minotaur lay wounded
and bleeding at the foot of my bed.

A sad creature,
dying,
the Minotaur came searching
for its beloved reward,
but I had already departed:
 "It is a shame
the things we love
go such ways wandering."

On this morning,
I emerged from the labyrinth,
determined
I would be the one to
sip the nectar of my blood,
gnaw the flesh of my soul.

~~~~~

Astral Dance

Staring into the sun
until sight is white nothing—
that's the gift I'm allowed.
Before, I don't recall.

Maybe I was a mystic,
a Merlin raising the dead,
confounding the masses
with sleights of hand.
Maybe I was Jack,
draining the life from
London whores.
Or is it possible I was
a prophet who saw
this day coming,
our inevitable end?

What would it have mattered?
What difference?

Tonight I shall drift
into white silence as
Pavarotti shrieks "Ave Maria"
through the headphones.

~~~~~

Trilogy in Stone

I

The aegis gleams
in visions
blinding;
her face,
damnation,
her eyes,
truth,
mirrors.
(I slew you
for no better reason than
whim.)

II

Your Sisters
yowl and hiss
at the brink
of conscience.
(Immortality whispers,
whispers,
"She has more
in death than we
everlasting.")
I touch the shield,
press my lips
to beauty
writhing.

III

(I kiss the soul;
the soul loves,
loves those who
kiss the soul.)
Image
is
stone
is
everlasting;
I shield my eyes
from the mirror,
my ears
from her mewls—
deflected nightmares in which

I

kiss

love

am

Stone.

~~~~~

Incarnations

The sun rises no brighter
above this island where all days begin.
Mist shimmers in saffron glow;
a raven glides over sienna waves
that bathe my toes on this matins beach.
I feel at peace here,
this place I've never been before,
this land where words are mysteries
and the sun does not matter more
than a cloud scattered on kind breezes.

She is shadow, desire, arms raised
like an angel's wings in the mist.
The raven angles against the current,
alights on driftwood slivers;
the angel folds her wings
and chants prayers against omens,
her breath tense, arms encircling,
soft, gracious, drawing in,
tears velvet against dusky skin.
I stare into the sun and envy the blind;
a voice, familiar as my own flesh,
whispers, *You're a good man.*

Driftwood splinters
into bare skin,
festering,
festering.
The breeze swirls, enfolds.
Arms arch,
angel taking flight,
breathless brush of fingertips,
a savoring of salt and birth,
and a promise to meet
on this beach another dawn
when ravens fail to circle
and angels weep mortal.

~~~~~

Apologies

Don't stand in the shadows.
Step out,
lay it down with all the rest—
yes, between the empties, if you like.

Never was good at it,
I admit—especially now,
at 2 a.m. when any man in his right mind
has tossed his ghosts into a grave
and closed his eyes for the night.
Jesus, I should have, wish I could have.

But all I could do was watch her chest
rise and fall, terrified it might stop,
and I'd be lying in the semi-darkness
of a bedroom on a steamy night like this,
alone.
Two hours, I endured,
then I came in here to sit among you.

Last night, I dreamed that she died,
but each evening she'd return, a specter,
and we'd talk about my day,
as if life were important.
And, once in the dream,
we made love, but I wasn't sure
if I had gone mad
or if it was real.

Yes, yes, you have a right to laugh.
You are figments after all,
with your faces frozen
in high school images,
but aged and wrinkled in life, I'm sure,
like mine,
all of you far beyond
conversations with inept ghosts like me
as I recall the times I could never say
I'm sorry.

Amen

Journey

We come from the myriad points we define,
searching for something we believe
can be found in rosaries and crosses,
in incense and chants,
in prayer and faith,
or buried behind the mosque,
underneath the cathedral,
among the glowing rocks
of the sweat-lodge;
and all the while,
all the while,
the gods themselves scream,
wake up, wake up,
yet we taste only
the hiccups of our breath,
feel the twitches of our intellect,
seeking, seeking, always seeking,
secretly afraid enlightenment
is a coil of rattlesnakes.

~~~~~

Predator

He's in the driveway, smile fixed,
swagger set, damn the no-soliciting sign.
From the garage,
I meet him at the sidewalk's edge.
The banter's light, friendly
as others approach neighboring houses,
recruiting.

Before he gets deep into it,
I tell him I'm not interested.
You attend church, look to God, right?

That's between God and me.
The smile falters.
He reaches for my shoulder, but I step back.
My friend, God has you in his sights.

That's the thing, I say,
turning back for the garage.
When did God become the predator?

~~~~~

Make-Believe

In this make-believe world,
I'll conjure a new god for us.
Give it any name you choose,
and we'll launch it
on autumn's decaying breeze.

Winds such as this draw
dark and desperate words,
echoes from those days of new jeans,
stiff, scratchy, two sizes too large,
cuffed and cycled
through wash after wash,
faded creases measuring
a season's growth,
waist frayed and tight by spring.
Autumn succumbed to screams
of winter nights, sobs and curses
that blamed each other,
prayers that roared for progeny
they could be proud of.
Winter's bitter wind fanned
hands, switches, belts
that raised welts
across lines of tears.
God knew all,
saw all from his
high, safe perch
in heaven—
that's what they said.
Yet god blocked not a single blow.

So name one in whom
we can confide all the good,

all the bad, all the fears and joy,
the beginning and in between.
If we convince ourselves,
if we simply fool ourselves into believing,
perhaps we'll coax heaven to swallow us
in the silence of our final breath.

~~~~~

Religion

Born Shinto, reared Buddhist,
she's found company in the Bible Belt,
leaving the question of falling trees
for the forest to resolve.
Husband and parents are
challenge enough,
the cascade of one eye,
one path, one saving grace.

And then, those Sunday mornings
that break with angry voices
over a daughter's need,
a mother's devotion,
a father's rights.

Speak softly a prayer,
please, please,
then silence.
And tears.

~~~~~

Was, Is

The stage is set with
PowerPoint and pamphlets,
certain to inform,
to nail the point home.
Crosses and whips and animated beatitudes,
thorns for the crown of logic,
dance across the screen and onto the sheet.

But, today, it all comes down
to the church marquee,
condemning through careful words,
and a hand rising in the far pew:
Didn't Jesus teach to accept, to nurture?

~~~~~

Key of G

In the beginning, God stood,
fingers snap, snap, snapping,
voice weaving a spell like
a billion chanting tongues.

When Gabriel raised his horn
and blew a melody true,
three sisters filled in harmony.

Word spread like ripples on water,
and now the group's got a gig
down on Bourbon Street;
there's even talk of a tour.
Their manager says
oldies are hot these days,
just go light on lyrics.

~~~~~

Flesh and Blood

None of us is ready when the wafers pass
the gum-chewing boy, eyes following indifferently.
Nevertheless, we each take one,
let it grow soggy and disintegrate
on the tongue,
wash it down with a shot of Welch's.

Both crackers and juice are reserved for
those who've braved the dunking pit
behind the pulpit, who've trusted
the preacher's plump, soft hands

to lift them before they've gulped
too much fetid water.

As the hint of grapes
clings to tongues,
the collection plate circulates,
gathering what it's all about
while the boy who loves Juicy Fruit
now dozes, head resting against his grandmother,
content to let god take care of itself.

Coda

For a Moment, I Shall

These shall remain:
the bouquet of roses;
the hymn of frogs;
the sun beyond frosted clouds;
the bite of mountain water;
the surge of gulf waves;
the claw of briars;
the call of owls in pre-dawn;
the silence of snow;
the patience of dirt.

These shall pass:
the self-taught trill of bamboo;
the resonance of strings;
the odor of skin;
the dampness of a single breath.

But until snow smothers memory,
each moment shall settle
like tea leaves in a cup,
savored in games of laughter,
illusions that leaves shall never dry.
Perhaps if I whisper to
the last leaf of experience,
the last drift of snow—
perhaps if I whisper, whisper.

~~~~~

Beauty

Beauty's a word
I've had little luck with,
although it's been tagged
to some of the trinkets I've created,
those dabbles at greatness,
those imitations of things greater, worthwhile,
but true beauty has always been
slightly out of reach—
dozens of good tries, but no cigars,

the search for the key ending
long before desire picked the lock,
the true beauty of pilgrimage blossoming
even when the pilgrim had begun to wither.

~~~~~

Autumn Grove
(originally entitled "History")

Autumn has arrived earlier than usual,
settling in this grove
of consolation and caresses.
I'm kicking up the past today,
crushing dead shoots
with each step.
When the wind blows
in Kyoto, she whispered,
bamboo sings.
Here, the breeze stirs
a clatter of bones.
Autumn clasps its frigid hand
around my heart.
She said true love lasts forever.
The bamboo moves.

~~~~~

Strains

The yard proved too much,
but not that first day when
weeds were tackled, trees trimmed, grass mowed,
and everything else cut to its place, good, proper, neat,
with time left for cleaning the garage and more.
Two days later with a simple twist,
he nearly collapsed.
Age, his friend laughed. *Next, you'll be fit for a box.*

In this small step,
this annoying pain,
the end.

Postal

You can pack months,
even years,
into an envelope.
One photo or a dozen,
it's all the same.
Stuff in a life,
slip it into transit,
and, on the other end,
they'll talk about birth
and pain and betrayal
and thumb through
lost generations
while life and death
arrive marked
Do Not Bend.

~~~~~

Leaves

Leaves bare their souls with color,
shed their attachments,
then drift on chilled, dry breezes.
It is the season that sets my eyes searching,
seeking the first glimpse of new green,
but days must run their course,
each birthing yet another *now*.
This is the way I wish to greet death:
Shedding burdens colored false and true,
drifting on fetal greens
that wash across oblivion.

~~~~~

The Odor of Dust

Believed the people
who said I was right,
and lit a candle

each night, caressed
him beside me.

Ran across the valleys
of his body until he lost
sight of darkness.
Cherished fingertips
that searched, probed
whatever it meant.

Left him wallowing
in empty sheets,
rooms and memories,
scribbled in a dusty corner;
savored the odor on my fingers.

Deny knowledge
for I can withstand
anonymity.
(And I never believe
the ones who say
it is wrong.)

~~~~~

Ringing Out the Old

Light slithers around poles
that stretch the tarpaulin tight,
casting grave shadows
across folding chairs
and folded faces.
Autumn hums in the backs of ears,
the old man's voice rasping distantly,
Take your seat, take your time;
it'll be over soon enough.

Melodies

We'll walk into this one again and again,
a tap on the top hat,
a tickle of strings,
and all that dirt.

She coaxes symphonies from soil and stone,
her garden sprouting double
with each passing year.
And I? I pluck songs from tradition,
strumming melodies reprised,
reprised still again,
refusing to see the end,
that coda she hums so softly,
unfettered, her fingers buried in soil,
dodging worms that could clean her bones.

She glances up,
a twitch of brow,
a gentle curve of lips,
and I see it all,
rushing headlong toward
that final measure,
that garden richness,
haunting even before
the final note of harvest
resonates to silence
and engulfs the last seed
planted.

~~~~~

Sea Roar

I despise shells
that ring the sea
in my ear:
I know it
for what it is.
I loathe the
sound my heart

beats through pillows
—a tender timpani,
walls stretched thin
against the sheets—
thump, thump, thump.
I'm certain
if I listen too long,
I will hear it stop.

~~~~~

I Was Young

A million years ago,
I kissed dew
from the petals of roses.

I was young once,
galloping through fields
as buds bared themselves to me.

A million years ago,
gentler skin caressed these hands—
when I was *young*.

The taste of dew lingers,
the gallop rocking me
ever onward,

alone,
even with all
I had.

He Said Wishes are as Good as Prayers, but His Friend has Walked a Thousand Dreams

Little more is left to do.
A walk.
A wish.
Speculation on dreams
and what could have been
if.
Kiss me.
Pull back slowly and smile.
Then, again,
the last time.
Hard.
Allow your fragrance
to bathe me once more.
Then turn quickly,
walk away.
I will linger here
a while longer.

C.S. Fuqua has worked as newspaper reporter, magazine editor, book editor, English tutor, substitute teacher, teacher aide, janitor, respiratory therapy technician, gas station attendant (when such things existed), salesclerk, and writing instructor, to name a few. He has been a full-time freelance writer since the mid-1980s, concentrating on fiction, nonfiction, and poetry. His hobbies include music and crafting Native American flutes which are sold through www.fluteflights.com.

Books by C.S. Fuqua:

White Trash & Southern, Collected Poems, Volume I
Notes to My Becca
The Native American Flute: Myth, History, Craft
Hush, Puppy! A Southern Fried Tale
Big Daddy's Fast-Past Gadget
Trust Walk
Rise Up
The Swing: Poems of Fatherhood
If I Were, I Would!
Deadlines audio novel series:
      Death in Service
      Deadlines
      Flight of the Omni
      Butterflies Die
Divorced Dads
Alabama Musicians: Musical Heritage from the Heart of Dixie
Music Fell on Alabama

Made in the USA
Middletown, DE
12 January 2017